The Language Experts

ENGLISH2.0

The Interactive Language Course for the 21st Century

APA Publications (UK) Limited

New York   London   Singapore

ENGLISH2.0

Contacting the Editors

Every effort has been made to provide accurate information in this publication, but changes are inevitable. The publisher cannot be responsible for any resulting loss, inconvenience or injury. We would appreciate it if readers would call our attention to any errors or outdated information by contacting Berlitz Publishing, e-mail: comments@berlitzpublishing.com

First Printing: June 2011
Printed in China

Publishing Director: Sheryl Olinsky Borg
Senior Editor/Project Manager: Lorraine Sova
Editorial: Andrea Pearman, Christine Condon, Paul Arcario,
Susan Stempleski, Lynne Strugnell
Cover and Interior Design: Leighanne Tillman
Interior Composition: Datagrafix, Inc.
Cover Photo: ©iStockphoto/ liaminou
Production Manager: Elizabeth Gaynor

Contents

How to Use ENGLISH2.0

ENGLISH2.0 is an innovative, beginner-level course that features a multimedia approach to help you function in a wide variety of everyday situations with English speakers. You'll practice [practise] listening, speaking, reading and writing in English online and by following the book.

 Visit the 2.0 companion website, **www.berlitzhotspot.com**, for all online and downloadable content.

ENGLISH2.0 is divided into 18 lessons. Each lesson focuses on an important theme, such as greetings, introductions, ordering food and shopping. The lessons include these features:

DIALOGUE

Real-life dialogues between native speakers of American English and British English

VOCABULARY

The lesson's key words and phrases

ACTIVITY

A fun way to practice [practise] your listening, speaking, reading and writing skills—in the book and online

DID YOU KNOW?

Cultural aspects of major English-speaking countries

GRAMMAR

Quick and easy grammar explanations

LEARNING TIP

Advice on how to learn English

PRONUNCIATION

A focus on the sounds of English

LEARN MORE

Practical ways to extend your language skills

 Check It!

A useful list of what you've accomplished in the lesson

BERLITZ HOTSPOT

Go to www.berlitzhotspot.com for...

 Social Networking
Prompts to start conversations
with your Hotspot friends

 Podcast
Downloadable information on British
and American culture and language

 Internet Activity
Explore real English websites

 User Guide
A translation of the 2.0 course
book, available in Spanish

 Video
Animated scenes of British and American gestures and situations

 Audio
For sections that are available with audio

Spellings and terms vary in American and British English. American spellings are used throughout this book, with the British spelling in square brackets where relevant, such as practice [practise], salesclerk [sales assistant]. You'll find two tests in the book, after lessons 9 and 18. The tests are an opportunity to confirm you've met the goals of the course. For your reference, an answer key has been included.

ENGLISH2.0 CD-ROM

 In addition to online content, 2.0 includes a CD-ROM, at the back of this book, with fun language-learning games, activities and audio. Practice [Practise] and reinforce the language you're learning!

Match It!
Play an English language
memory game.

Quiz2.0
Test your knowledge of
the English language and
its grammar and culture.

Watch It!
Answer questions about
the English2.0 videos.

Listen Up!
Advance your listening
comprehension skills.

Speak Up!
Practice [Practise] your
English pronunciation.

Pronunciation

This section is designed to make you familiar with the sounds of English using the International Phonetic Alphabet (IPA) symbols. The IPA consists of a set of symbols in which one symbol always represents one sound.

CONSONANTS

Phonetic Symbol	Typical Spellings	Initial Position	Middle Position	Final Position
[s]	s, ss, c	sit	missing	face
[z]	z, zz	zoo	lazy	buzz
[t]	t	toe	return	hat
[d]	d	day	ladder	head
[θ]	th	thumb	author	bath
[ð]	th	them	mother	breathe
[ʃ]	sh, ss	she	tissue	fish
[tʃ]	ch, tu, tch	cherry	nature	watch
[ʒ]	si, ge	-	vision	beige
[dʒ]	j, g, dg	jello [jelly]	magic	edge
[j]	y	yes	mayor	-
[p]	p	pot	happy	tip
[b]	b	boy	table	cab
[f]	f	fun	after	if
[v]	v	very	oven	dive
[k]	c, ck, k	coat	package	like
[g]	g, gg	give	ago	egg
[w]	w	wet	away	-
[l]	l, ll	love	hello	pill
[r]	r, rr	rock	merry	car

4

Phonetic Symbol	Typical Spellings	Initial Position	Middle Position	Final Position
[h]	h	<u>h</u>it	be<u>h</u>ind	-
[m]	m, mm	<u>m</u>y	ha<u>mm</u>er	fa<u>m</u>e
[n]	n, nn	<u>n</u>ot	fu<u>nn</u>y	i<u>n</u>
[ŋ]	ng	-	si<u>ng</u>er	thi<u>ng</u>

VOWELS

Phonetic Symbol	Typical Spellings	Initial Position	Middle Position	Final Position
[i]	e, ee, ea, ie	<u>e</u>ven	t<u>ea</u>m	s<u>ee</u>
[ɪ]	i, ui, y	<u>i</u>t	qu<u>i</u>ck	-
[eɪ]	a, ay, ai	<u>a</u>te	p<u>ai</u>d	aw<u>ay</u>
[ɛ]	e, ea	<u>e</u>gg	h<u>ea</u>d	-
[æ]	a	<u>a</u>pple	h<u>a</u>t	-
[a]	a, o	<u>o</u>pera	f<u>a</u>ther	-
[u]	u, oo, ew, u	-	m<u>oo</u>n	y<u>ou</u>
[ʊ]	u, ou	-	p<u>u</u>t	-
[ʌ]	u	<u>u</u>p	s<u>o</u>me	-
[oʊ]	o, oa, ough	<u>o</u>h	c<u>oa</u>t	th<u>ough</u>
[ɔ]	a, aw	<u>a</u>ll	cr<u>aw</u>l	s<u>aw</u>
[ə]	a	<u>a</u>bove	op<u>e</u>n	sod<u>a</u>
[ɚ]	er, or	-	p<u>er</u>haps	col<u>or</u> [colour]
[ɝ]	ear, or, ur	<u>ear</u>n	w<u>or</u>k	f<u>ur</u>
[aʊ]	ou, ow	<u>ou</u>t	m<u>ou</u>se	n<u>ow</u>
[aɪ]	i, igh, y	b<u>i</u>te	s<u>igh</u>	sk<u>y</u>
[ɔɪ]	oi, oy	<u>oi</u>l	c<u>oi</u>n	t<u>oy</u>

Lesson 1

Meeting and Greeting

LESSON OBJECTIVES

Lesson 1 is about getting to know people.
After you finish this lesson, you'll know how to:

- exchange greetings
- introduce yourself
- spell

DIALOGUE

Listen to these people greet each other.

1.

Man:	**Morning, Sue.**
Woman:	**Oh, hi Joe. How are you?**
Man:	**Pretty good, thanks. And you?**
Woman:	**Yes, I'm fine, thanks. Nice car.**
Man:	**Thanks.**

2.

Woman:	**Good afternoon.**
Man:	**Oh, hello. I'm Nick Roberts.**
Woman:	**Ah, yes. Mr. Roberts. Just a moment, please.**
Man:	**Thank you.**

3.

Man 1:	**OK, Tom. Goodbye.**
Man 2:	**Goodbye, Mr. Smith. And thanks.**
Man 1:	**That's OK. Good night.**

4.

Man:	**Hello. Mr. and Mrs. Grant?**
Woman:	**Yes, that's right.**
Man:	**Good evening. This is your table.**
Woman:	**Thank you.**

1. DIALOGUE ACTIVITY

What are some of the greetings you heard?

Example: Hi.

Use the following words and expressions to guide you through the lesson.

VOCABULARY

afternoon

and

bye (short form of goodbye)

car

coffee

Could you repeat that?

evening (from 6pm to 10pm)

fine

first name

Good afternoon.

Good evening.

Good morning.

Good night. (use this to say goodbye)

Goodbye.

Hello.

Hi. (informal version of hello)

How are you?

I'm fine.

(I'm) sorry? (use this when you don't hear or understand what someone said)

just a moment

last name/surname

late

Mr. (title for an adult man)

Mrs. (title for a married woman)

Ms. (title for any adult woman)

My name is...

Nice to meet you.

no

okay/OK

Pardon? (In British English, use this when you didn't hear what someone said)

Pardon?/Excuse me? (use this when you don't hear or understand what someone said)

please

pretty good/well

See you! (use this to say goodbye)

Sorry! (an apology)

table

thank you

thanks (short form of thank you)

that

that's right

this

What's your name?

yes

Hello.

How are you?

DID YOU KNOW?

There are over 300 million English native speakers worldwide.

2. LISTENING ACTIVITY

Listen to the four short conversations again. Write the number of the conversation under the correct picture.

a. [ ]

b. [ ]

c. [1]

d. [ ]

3. LISTENING ACTIVITY

Mr. Bechstein arrives at his hotel to check in. Listen to the conversation and fill in the blanks. (There is one space for each missing word.) Then listen to check your answers. The first one is done for you.

Clerk: [Good] [afternoon.]

Guest: [ ] afternoon. [ ]

[ ] is Christian Bechstein.

Clerk: I'm [ ], could you repeat that, [ ] ?

Guest: Christian Bechstein. [ ] [ ] name

is Christian, and [ ] [ ] name

[ ] Bechstein.

Clerk: Ah, yes, Mr. Bechstein. [ ] [ ] .

10

4. LISTENING ACTIVITY

 Now listen to four people spell their names. Number the names in the order you hear them.

T. Bisset		**M. Campana**	1
G. Chaplin		**P. Massey**	

5. LISTENING ACTIVITY

Listen to the pronunciation of the English alphabet.

English
Alphabet

A B C D E F G

H I J K L M N

O P Q R S T U

V W X Y Z

DID YOU KNOW?

In English-speaking countries it is very common for people to have three names: a first name, a middle name and a last name. In most situations, people use their first and last names. They usually use middle names in formal documents.

6. **LISTENING ACTIVITY**

Listen to the spelling of three women's first names and three men's first names. Write them in the spaces provided. The first one is done for you.

1. **Susan**

2.

3.

4.

5.

6.

Now, can you spell them out loud?

DID YOU KNOW?

In English-speaking countries, many married women take their husband's last names. A woman's last name that she used from birth is known as her *maiden name*.

7. **SPEAKING ACTIVITY**

Introduce yourself. Use the model: *Hello, I'm (insert your name)*. Then, practice [practise] spelling your name and your close friends' and family members' names aloud.

The Present Tense of the Verb to Be — GRAMMAR

In English, the verb *to be* is an irregular verb. Notice that the forms of *to be* are often contracted, or shortened, with the pronouns (I, you, he, she, etc.):

Full Form (Pronoun + Verb)	Contracted Form
I am	I'm
you are	you're
he is	he's
she is	she's
it is	it's
we are	we're
you are	you're
they are	they're

Hello, I'm Sue Fisher.

We're sorry.

They're late.

He's fine. (Tom is fine.)

8. WRITING ACTIVITY

Write the full forms for each contracted form of *to be*.

1. **they're**   they are
2. **she's**
3. **we're**
4. **I'm**
5. **you're**
6. **he's**
7. **it's**

Not

GRAMMAR

To make a verb negative, use the word *not*.

I am not Sue Fisher./I'm not Sue Fisher.

Not also has the contracted form *n't*.

We aren't sorry.

For *I am* the negative forms are the following:

I am not.   I'm not.

Note that you can only use one contracted form at a time. If *not* is contracted, then the verb is not contracted.

✔ *She's not*   ✔ *She isn't*   ✘ *She's isn't*

---

9. SPEAKING ACTIVITY

Say the contracted form for each of the full forms of *to be*. Then spell each aloud.

1. **I am**

2. **we are**

3. **you are**

4. **he is**

5. **they are**

6. **it is**

7. **she is**

10. WRITING ACTIVITY

Write these forms of *to be* in the negative, using the full form of *not*.

1. **they're**   they are not
2. **she's**
3. **we're**
4. **I'm**
5. **you're**
6. **he's**
7. **it's**

11. WRITING ACTIVITY

Write the forms of *to be* in the negative. Use the contracted form of *not*.

1. **they're**   they aren't
2. **she's**
3. **we're**
4. **I'm**
5. **you're**
6. **he's**
7. **it's**

Possessive adjectives show that an object belongs to someone or something.

Subject	Possessive Adjective
I	my
you	your
he	his
she	her
it	its (animal or object)
we	our
you (plural)	your (plural)
they	their

His name is Tom.   That's my coffee!   Her name is Susan.

Note: The third person (his/her) agrees with the gender of the possessor:

Paul took his suitcase. (*Paul* is masculine.)

Susan took her suitcase. (*Susan* is feminine.)

Add *'s* to a person's name to show possession.

Judy's last name is Wells.

12. WRITING ACTIVITY

For each pair of pictures, write the name of the object and the correct possessive adjective. Then write the correct form using 's with the person's name.

Jack

1.
his coffee, Jack's coffee

Mary and Elizabeth

2.

Caroline

3.

John

4.

Check It!

Test what you learned in this lesson. Review anything you're not sure of.

CAN YOU . . . ?

☐ **greet someone in the morning, afternoon and evening**
Good morning.
Good afternoon.
Good evening.
Hello./Hi.

☐ **say goodbye to someone**
Goodbye./Bye.
Good night.
See you!

☐ **introduce yourself**
Hello, I'm Nick Roberts.

☐ **ask how someone is**
How are you?

☐ **say the forms of *to be***
I am, you are, he/she/it is, we are, they are

☐ **use the contracted forms of *to be***
I'm, you're, he's/she's/it's, we're, they're

☐ **make the forms of *to be* negative**
I am not/I'm not
you are not/you're not/you aren't
he is not/he's not/he isn't, she is not/she's not/she isn't, it is not/it's not/it isn't
we are not/we're not/we aren't
they are not/they're not/they aren't

☐ **give your name**
My name's Bill Waits.
I'm Sue Fisher.
My first name is Bill, and my last name is Waits.

☐ **spell your name**

BERLITZ HOTSPOT   Go to www.berlitzhotspot.com for...

 Social Networking
Meet the Berlitz Barista and make new friends learning English just like you. Share what you learned, ask questions, trade tips, find photos and more!

 Podcast 1
Informal Greetings
Download this podcast.

 Internet Activity
Are you interested in learning more English names? Go to **Berlitz Hotspot** for a list of sites of popular English names. Browse and pick three or four names you like. Say and spell the names aloud. Make up simple sentences like: *My name is..., Her name is...,* etc.

 Video 1 – How Do You Do?
Two people are meeting each other for the first time. What do they say? What do they do? Watch the video and find out how to greet English speakers.

Lesson 2

How Are You?

LESSON OBJECTIVES

Lesson 2 is about meeting people. After you finish this lesson, you'll know how to:

- meet new people
- introduce others
- ask for and give information about names, nationalities and cities

DIALOGUE

 Listen to two friends on a plane as they talk to the person sitting next to them.

Bob: **Sorry!**

Maria: **It's OK. It's OK.**

Bob: **My name's Bob, Bob Stewart.**

Maria: **Nice to meet you. I'm Maria Garcia.**

Bob: **Pleased to meet you, Maria. And this is my friend Tony, Tony Davies.**

Tony: **How do you do?**

Maria: **How do you do?**

Bob: **So, where are you from, Maria? You're not British . . .**

Maria: **No, I'm not. I'm from Spain. And you? Are you British?**

Bob: **Yes, we both are. I'm from Scotland and Tony's from Wales.**

1. DIALOGUE ACTIVITY

What are the names of the people in the dialogue?

a. Garcia

b.

c.

Where are they from?

a. Spain

b.

c.

20

Use the following words and expressions to guide you through the lesson.

VOCABULARY

America/United States of America

both

Britain

British (a person or thing from Britain)

Canada

Canadian (a person or thing from Canada)

England

English (the language and a person or thing from England)

everyone

Excuse me.

France

French (the language and a person or thing from France)

friend

from

How are you?/How do you do?

Italian (the language and a person or thing from Italy)

Italy

Japan

Japanese (the language and a person or thing from Japan)

Mexico

Mexican (a person or thing from Mexico)

next

Nice to meet you./Pleased to meet you.

North American

Scotland

Scottish (a person or thing from Scotland)

Spain

Spanish (the language and a person or thing from Spain)

team

This is...

Wales

welcome

Welsh (a person or thing from Wales)

what

Where are you from?

GRAMMAR

Capitalization

In English certain words are always written with a capital letter, for example, the names of people, countries, cities and nationalities; the first word of a sentence; the word *I*.

I am French.

Philip is from Boston.

He is in Spain.

2. LISTENING ACTIVITY

 Listen to Activity 1 again. Write if the sentences are true or false.

1. **Tony is from Scotland.** `false`

2. **Maria isn't Spanish.**

3. **Tony is Bob's friend.**

4. **Bob and Tony are British.**

3. WRITING ACTIVITY

Read the sentences about people in a competition. Circle the letters that should be capitalized.

1. (h)ello. (m)y name's (k)enji (m)atsuda and (i)'m from (t)okyo.

2. this is tom priest, and he's canadian.

3. good evening. i'm henri bernard and i'm from france.

4. gina isn't spanish she's italian.

5. is rosa from brazil?

DID YOU KNOW?

 The island of Great Britain is made up of three countries, England, Scotland and Wales—so English, Scottish and Welsh people are all *British*. Great Britain and Northern Ireland together are the United Kingdom, or U.K. for short.

The term *North American* refers to anyone from North America: the United States or Canada. *Central American* refers to people from any of the countries of Central America and *South American* refers to anyone from South America.

You can say that a native speaker of English is an *English speaker*.

4. READING ACTIVITY

Bill Waits has an appointment with Sue Fisher. They meet in the reception area of her office. Complete the conversation.

Sue: **Excuse me,** [are] [you] **Mr. Waits?**

Smith: **No,** [ ] **name's Smith.**

Sue: **Oh, I'm** [ ]**!**

Sue: **Excuse me, Mr. Waits?**

Bill: **Yes,** [ ] [ ] **Bill Waits.**

Sue: **How** [ ] [ ]**, Mr. Waits? Sue Fisher.**

Bill: **Pleased** [ ] [ ] [ ]**.**

23

5. SPEAKING ACTIVITY

Give a reasonable answer to each question.

1. **Is he well?**

   Yes, he's well.

2. **Where are you from?**

3. **Is he from London?**

4. **Are they American?**

5. **Excuse me, are you Sue Fisher?**

6. **How are you? I'm Mike Smith.**

GRAMMAR

To form a question, place the verb before the subject. Note that this is the opposite of a statement, where the subject comes before the verb. Look at the examples below:

Statements	Questions
You are from Liverpool.	Are you from Liverpool?
He is from Canada.	Is he from Canada?

For a negative question, use the contracted form, rather than the full form of *not*.

They are not from New York.   Aren't they from New York?

6. SPEAKING ACTIVITY

Imagine you are traveling [travelling] with a friend and meet another person. Use the following hints to help you start a conversation.

- **greet the person**
- **say your name**
- **say where you are from (country, city or nationality)**
- **introduce your friend**
- **say where your friend is from**

Example:

> How do you do? My name's Judy Wells. I'm English. I'm from Liverpool. This is Tom Anderson. He's from Canada.

GRAMMAR

Simple yes/no questions can be answered using short answer forms. These are the short answer forms:

Yes, I am.	No, I'm not.
Yes, we/you/they are.	No, we/you/they aren't.
Yes, he/she/it is.	No, he/she/it isn't.

Note: You can only use contracted forms for negatives in short answers.

Are Mr. and Mrs. Grant from Canada?

✔ Yes, they are.   ✗ Yes, they're.

Is your car Japanese? No, it isn't.

Are you Judy Wells? Yes, I am.

Is Tom North American? Yes, he is.

7. WRITING ACTIVITY

Change the following statements into questions.

1. **Philip is from New York.**   **Is Philip from New York?**

2. **She is in Spain.**

3. **They are from Brazil.**

4. **I am from France.**

5. **We are in London.**

6. **You are not Emma Harris.**

8. WRITING ACTIVITY

Give short answers to the following questions in the affirmative and the negative.

	Yes, he is.	No, he isn't.
1. **Is he Tony's friend?**		
2. **Are you Spanish?**		
3. **Are they from the U.S.?**		
4. **Are we in Liverpool?**		
5. **Is she Italian?**		
6. **Am I English?**		

9. WRITING ACTIVITY

Rearrange the words to make a correct statement.

1. **French/car/is/his.**	His car is French.
2. **name/first/Emma/is/her.**	
3. **not/we/are/Italy/from.**	
4. **Jack's/Tom/is/friend.**	
5. **from/aren't/we/North America.**	

10. WRITING ACTIVITY

Rearrange the words to make a correct question.

1. **David's/is/car/that?**

   Is that David's car?

2. **are/Spanish/you?**

3. **from/are/we/Japan?**

4. **she/John's/is/friend?**

5. **last/Judy's/Waits/name/is?**

11. READING ACTIVITY

You receive some emails from friends who are just learning English. Correct their mistakes.

SEND   **DELETE**

To:

From: pablo@pablito.com

Subject: Hello!

H
hello. How are you? My name Pablo. Where you are from? I from Madrid in Spain

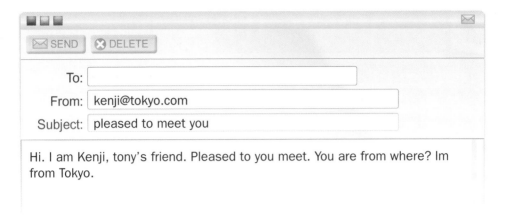

To:
From: kenji@tokyo.com
Subject: pleased to meet you

Hi. I am Kenji, tony's friend. Pleased to you meet. You are from where? Im from Tokyo.

12. ACTIVITY

Complete the word search.

J	A	P	A	N	E	S	E	E	O	F	H
G	O	O	D	B	Y	E	W	E	N	S	T
G	M	E	X	I	C	A	N	O	I	E	H
M	O	R	N	I	N	G	O	L	I	V	A
C	A	K	X	N	Z	N	G	I	C	E	N
A	E	M	B	F	R	N	E	D	I	N	K
N	M	N	E	E	E	E	O	E	T	I	Y
A	E	A	T	R	N	R	R	T	A	N	O
D	O	F	F	I	I	A	N	E	L	G	U
I	A	C	A	N	K	C	M	E	I	B	A
A	F	R	E	N	C	H	A	E	A	G	W
N	S	P	A	N	I	S	H	N	N	N	I

afternoon	evening	Japanese	Spanish
American	French	Mexican	thank you
Canadian	goodbye	morning	
English	Italian	name	

Check It!

Test what you learned in this lesson. Review anything you're not sure of.

CAN YOU . . . ?

☐ **introduce yourself**
I'm Bob Stewart.
My name is Bob Stewart.

☐ **introduce a friend**
This is my friend Tony Davies.

☐ **say where you or someone else is from**
I am from Spain.
He is from Wales.

☐ **state your nationality or someone else's**
I am Mexican.
She is French.

☐ **say a number of country names**
Brazil
France
Italy
Japan
Mexico

☐ **ask simple questions**
Is Tony from Scotland?
Are you from New York?

☐ **give short answers to questions**
Yes, I am./No, I am not./No, I'm not.
Yes, he is./No, he is not./No, he's not./No, he isn't.

BERLITZ HOTSPOT   Go to www.berlitzhotspot.com for...

Social Networking
Go to **Berlitz Hotspot** and introduce yourself. Use this model: *Hi, my name is (your name). I'm from (your location).*

Podcast 2
No Kissing!
Download this podcast.

Internet Activity
Learn more country names and nationalities. Go to **Berlitz Hotspot** for a list of sites with maps in English. Practice making questions or statements about the countries and their residents, like *Are you from Australia?* or *Nikos is from Greece.*

Lesson 3

My Number Is...

DIALOGUE

Listen to some people asking for phone extension numbers and room numbers.

1.

Woman:	**Good morning. Delta Engineering.**
Man:	**Oh, good morning. Extension two, four, seven, please.**
Woman:	**Two, four, seven. Just a moment, please.**

2.

Woman:	**Hello. Is this eight, eight, two, five?**
Man:	**Yes, that's right. Eight, eight, two, five.**
Woman:	**Oh, hello. This is Sue Fisher.**

3.

Man:	**Room number nine-oh-six, please.**
Woman:	**I'm sorry?**
Man:	**Nine-oh-six, please.**
Woman:	**Just a moment, please.**

4.

Man:	**My name's Bill Waits and my extension number is seven, zero, four, one.**
Woman:	**I'm sorry. Could you repeat that, please?**
Man:	**Seven, zero, four, one.**
Woman:	**Thank you.**

1. DIALOGUE ACTIVITY

You heard some numbers in the dialogue. How many numbers from 0 to 9 do you already know in English?

Use the following words and expressions to guide you through the lesson.

VOCABULARY

a.m. (time between midnight and noon)

extension

extension number

in the evening

in the morning

new

number

o'clock

p.m. (time between noon and midnight)

repeat, to

room

telephone/phone

the

What time is it?

zero (usually read as *oh* in a phone number)

---

2. **LISTENING ACTIVITY**

 Listen to the numbers from zero to nine.

0	zero	4	four	8	eight
1	one	5	five	9	nine
2	two	6	six		
3	three	7	seven		

Now listen to the dialogue again. Circle the numbers you hear.

1. **257**   (**247**)   **249**

2. **8825**   **9925**   **8829**

3. **706**   **916**   **906**

4. **7401**   **7041**   **7014**

DID YOU KNOW?

The standard greeting when answering a telephone in English is "hello."

Hello!

3. LISTENING ACTIVITY

Listen to some messages on an answering machine. What are the telephone numbers? Write them down.

1. **Joe Carter** — 555–9841
2. **BBA Limited**
3. **Judy Wells**
4. **Delta Engineering**

Hi, Sue. How are you? This is Joe, Joe Carter. My new telephone number, it's five, five, five, nine, eight, four, one. See you! Bye.

This is BBA Limited. Our new telephone number is five, five, five, eight, four, nine, zero. Thank you.

Bill? This is Judy, Judy Wells. This is my new number. It's five, five, five, one, seven, zero, three. OK? Five, five, five, one, seven, zero, three. Bye!

Hello, this is Delta Engineering. Our new number is five, five, five, two, nine, four, one. Thank you.

4. SPEAKING ACTIVITY

Look at your answers to Activity 3. Read the information using the following model: *This is (insert name). My/our number is (insert number)*, as in the example.

Example:

This is Joe, Joe Carter. My number is five, five, five, nine, eight, four, one.

5. LISTENING ACTIVITY

 You need to call a company called Thomas Travel to speak to Mr. Bill Massey. Follow the prompts below to complete the conversation. Then turn on the recording and wait for him to speak.

Massey: **Hello, Thomas Travel.**

You: Ask if this is Mr. Massey.

Massey: **Yes, it is. This is Bill Massey.**

You: Greet him, and tell him who you are.

Massey: **I'm sorry, could you repeat that, please?**

You: Repeat your name again.

Massey: **Ah, good morning. How are you?**

DID YOU KNOW?

 When you give times in English like 1:00, 2:00, 3:00, etc., you can say the hour (1 through [to] 12) then say *o'clock*. This is followed by either *in the morning* or *a.m.*, or *in the evening* or *p.m.* American English does not use the 24-hour clock and in British English the 24-hour clock is not usually used in conversation.

6. WRITING ACTIVITY

 Listen to people ask the time in different places. Then look at the clocks below and write the name of the city or country next to each clock.

a.

a.m.

c.

a.m.

 b.

New York

p.m.

Man:	**Excuse me.**
Woman:	**Yes, can I help you?**
Man:	**What time is it, please?**
Woman:	**It's twelve o'clock.**
Man:	**And what time is it in New York?**
Woman:	**In New York? It's eight p.m.**
Man:	**Thank you.**

Woman:	**Hello, can I help you?**
Man:	**Yes, what time is it in Tokyo, please?**
Woman:	**It's ten a.m.**
Man:	**Ten o'clock. Thank you.**

Man:	**Hello, is that Jane?**
Woman:	**Yes, this is Jane.**
Man:	**Hi, it's Tom.**
Woman:	**Tom? Tom! Hi!**
Man:	**What time is it in England?**
Woman:	**One o'clock in the morning!**
Man:	**Oh, sorry!**
Woman:	**It's OK.**

Prepositions

GRAMMAR

Use *in* to talk about time: in the morning, in the afternoon, in the evening.

> It's 3:00 (three o'clock) in the morning.

> Is it 7:00 (seven o'clock) in the evening?

In also shows location: a city or country.

> What time is it in Tokyo?

> It's 5:00 (five o'clock) in Rome.

DID YOU KNOW?

The Prime Meridian at Greenwich (a suburb of London) is the name given to the reference line for world time. Time zones to the west of the Prime Meridian are up to 12 hours behind and time zones to the east are up to 12 hours ahead. So, for example, while people in London are looking forward to eating lunch, people in New York are just waking up and people in Sydney are getting ready for bed.

DID YOU KNOW?

The United States has four different time zones.

7. [SPEAKING   ACTIVITY] **"**

 Now it's your turn to leave a message. Here are some hints to help you.
First listen to the example, then you try. You may wish to practice [practise]
by writing down your answer, below.

- **greet the person**
- **say your name**
- **spell your first name**
- **spell your last name**
- **give your telephone number**
- **give the time**
- **say goodbye**

Example: Good morning. This is Etsuko Matsui. My first name is Etsuko.
E - T - S - U - K - O. And my last name is Matsui. M - A - T - S - U - I. My telephone
number is five, five, five, two, five, zero, five. And it's ten o'clock in the morning.
Thank you.

Word Stress

PRONUNCIATION

The stressed syllable in a word is the syllable that you hear as being the loudest and longest.

Say the word *number*. Notice that the syllable "num" is louder and longer than "ber." Though many English words follow a stressed-unstressed pattern, like *number*, it is not always easy to guess where the stress falls in an English word. The following exercises will help you recognize the stressed syllables.

8. LISTENING ACTIVITY

Listen to some examples of word stress. Underline the stressed part of the word. The first one has been done for you.

<u>eve</u>ning	number
sorry	goodbye
good night	Mexico
morning	hello
telephone	Portugal

9. LISTENING ACTIVITY

Listen to the pairs of words. Say if the stress in the two words is the same or different.

English, morning   same

Italy, Japanese

goodbye, seven

telephone, Canada

hello, number

LEARNING TIP

Don't try to do too much at one time. Study for short periods every day and review often. Try to set a regular time to study.

Check It!

Test what you learned in this lesson. Review anything you're not sure of.

CAN YOU . . . ?

- [ ] **answer the telephone**
  Hello?

- [ ] **ask for an extension or a room number**
  Extension two, four, seven, please.
  Room number nine-oh-six, please.

- [ ] **say who you are when leaving a message and give your phone number**
  This is (your name). My number is (your telephone number).

- [ ] **ask what time it is**
  What time is it in Tokyo?

- [ ] **say the time**
  It's 3:00 (three o'clock) in the morning.
  Is it 7:00 (seven o'clock) in the evening?

- [ ] **use *in* to show location with a city or country**
  It's 10 p.m. in New York.

- [ ] **identify word stress when you hear a word**

Learn More ✚

Do you sometimes read English language newspapers or magazines? If so, look at the foreign news section. See how many country names you know. You can do the same thing when you hear English on TV or on the radio.

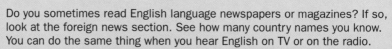 **BERLITZ HOTSPOT**   Go to www.berlitzhotspot.com for...

 Social Networking
Go to **Berlitz Hotspot** and share your thoughts on what you learned in this lesson, like English word stress. Do you have any funny pronunciation stories? Share them with your Hotspot friends.

 Podcast 3
My Number Is...
Download this podcast.

 Internet Activity
For more practice with phone numbers, go to **Berlitz Hotspot** for a link to the American phonebook. Try a few searches and make simple sentences using the information you find.

 Video 2 – A Business Call
A businesswoman calls a travel agency. What does she say to the receptionist who answers the phone? How does the businesswoman leave a message? Watch the video and learn how to make a business call in English.

Lesson 4

Buying Food and Drink

LESSON OBJECTIVES

Lesson 4 is about ordering food and drink. When you finish this lesson, you'll know how to:

- order something to eat or drink
- ask for prices

DIALOGUE

 Listen to two people ordering in a coffee shop.

Customer 2:	**Hi.**
Customer 1:	**Morning, Tom. How are you?**
Customer 2:	**Fine, thanks.**
Waitress:	**Good morning. What would you like?**
Customer 1:	**Um, I'd like a cup of coffee, please.**
Customer 2:	**And I'll have tea.**
Waitress:	**Milk or lemon?**
Customer 2:	**Milk, please.**
Waitress:	**Here you are.**

1. DIALOGUE ACTIVITY

What does each person order?

DID YOU KNOW?

Coffee is the most popular hot drink in the United States and Canada. Tea is more popular in the U.K., but many people also drink tea in the U.S. and Canada.

Tap water is free in American and British restaurants.

42

Use the following words and expressions to guide you through the lesson.

a/an	lemon
altogether	milk
cent	mineral water
cola	omelet [omelette]
cup	or
cup of coffee	orange juice
dollar	pastry
fruit salad	pence
green salad	(baked) potato
grilled [toasted] cheese sandwich	pound (British currency/a unit of weight, shortened to "lb.")
hamburger	
Here you are.	soda
hot dog	sugar
How much...?	tea
ice cream	tuna sandwich
iced tea	water
I'd like...	What would you like?
I'll have...	

2. **LISTENING ACTIVITY**

 Listen to some more people order refreshments. On the menu, number the items from 1 to 7 in the order you hear them. The first one has been done for you.

DID YOU KNOW?

 The currency in the U.S., Canada, Australia and New Zealand is in dollars and cents, but in Britain it is in pounds and pence. Pence is shortened to *p* (pronounced "pee"), so instead of saying *60 pence*, the British say *60p*. For items costing more than £1, it is usual just to say, for example, *one pound 25*, not *one pound 25p*.

Menu

	Hot Dog	$1.95
	Hamburger	$3.75
	Tuna Sandwich	$2.75
1	Omelet	$3.25
	Grilled Cheese Sandwich	$3.25
	Green Salad	$3.75
	Orange Juice	$2.25
	Soda	$2.00
	Iced Tea	$2.00
	Mineral Water	$2.25
	Coffee	$1.50

3. WRITING ACTIVITY

Look at the menu again. Write down the name of each item with the indefinite article *a* or *an*. Listen to the recording of Activity 2 again to check your answers.

1. **an omelet [omelette]**

2.

3.

4.

5.

6.

7.

Menu

Hot Dog	$1.95
Hamburger	$3.75
Tuna Sandwich	$2.75
Omelet	$3.25
Grilled Cheese Sandwich	$3.25
Green Salad	$3.75
Orange Juice	$2.25
Soda	$2.00
Iced Tea	$2.00
Mineral Water	$2.25
Coffee	$1.50

GRAMMAR

The indefinite article (*a/an*) is used to refer to a noun in a general sense. It can often be replaced by the number *one*. The English indefinite article has two forms, *a* and *an*.

Use *a* before a consonant sound:

I'd like a hamburger, please.

I'll have a tuna sandwich.

Use *an* before a vowel sound:

I'd like an orange juice.

It's an MP3 player. (MP3 is pronounced "em-pee-three")

Now that you know the rule, go back and correct your answers for Activity 3.

4. SPEAKING ACTIVITY

Look at the three coffee shop checks [bills]. What did the people say when they ordered?

Example: I'd like a hamburger and an iced tea, please.

JOE'S

1	Toasted Cheese Sandwich	£ 3.25
1	Tea	£ 1.25

Total £ 4.50

JOE'S

1	Baked Potato with Cheese	£ 4.95
1	Coffee	£ 1.75
1	Mineral Water	£ 1.25

Total £ 7.95

JOE'S

1	Omelette	£ 3.75
1	Orange Juice	£ 0.95

Total £ 4.70

5. SPEAKING ACTIVITY

Practice [practise] saying some numbers from 11 to 100 aloud.

11	eleven	21	twenty-one	20	twenty
12	twelve	22	twenty-two	30	thirty
13	thirteen	23	twenty-three	40	forty
14	fourteen	24	twenty-four	50	fifty
15	fifteen	25	twenty-five	60	sixty
16	sixteen	26	twenty-six	70	seventy
17	seventeen	27	twenty-seven	80	eighty
18	eighteen	28	twenty-eight	90	ninety
19	nineteen	29	twenty-nine	100	one hundred

6. LISTENING ACTIVITY

 Listen to some customers in a coffee shop ask how much things cost. Fill in the prices on the check [bill].

Customer 1: Excuse me, how much is the pastry?

Clerk 1: It's two seventy-five.

Customer 1: And how much is a coffee?

Clerk 1: A dollar fifty.

....

Customer 2: What does the soda cost?

Clerk 2: Ninety-five cents.

Customer 2: And the sandwich? How much is the grilled toasted cheese sandwich?

Clerk 2: It's three twenty-five.

....

Customer 1: Excuse me. How much do I owe you?

Clerk 1: One fruit salad, three ninety-five.... one mineral water, two twenty-five..., and an ice cream, two dollars. That's eight dollars and twenty cents, please.

Check	
Sally's Diner	
Pastry	$2.75
Grilled Cheese Sandwich	$
Fruit Salad	$
Soda	$
Coffee	$
Mineral Water	$
Ice Cream	$
Total	$

People say *would like*… to ask politely for something they want.

I would like a soda.

In spoken English, *would* in affirmative statements is usually contracted to *'d*:

I'd like an omelet [omelette]. = I would like an omelet [omelette].

He'd like a new car. = He would like a new car.

Questions use the full form *would*:

What would you like?

7. SPEAKING ACTIVITY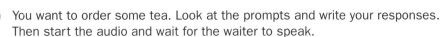

You want to order some tea. Look at the prompts and write your responses. Then start the audio and wait for the waiter to speak.

Waiter:	**Can I help you?**
You:	Ask for some tea.
Waiter:	**Milk or lemon?**
You:	Say which you prefer.
Waiter:	**Here you are.**
You:	Ask how much it is.
Waiter:	**That's ninety-five cents.**

DID YOU KNOW?

In an American restaurant, the written list of what you owe is called a *check*, but in Britain it's called a *bill*.

Check It!

Test what you learned in this lesson. Review anything you're not sure of.

CAN YOU . . . ?

☐ **order food or drink**
I'd like a cup of coffee, please.
I'll have tea.

☐ **use the indefinite article**
I'd like a hamburger and an iced tea.

☐ **say the numbers between 11 and 100**

☐ **ask for prices**
Excuse me, how much is the pastry?
And how much is a coffee?

☐ **use *would like* and its contracted forms**
I'd like an omelet [omelette].
What would you like?

BERLITZ HOTSPOT   Go to www.berlitzhotspot.com for...

Social Networking
Tell your Hotspot friends about your favorite [favourite] American or English foods or drinks.

Podcast 4
Let's Get Takeout!
Download this podcast.

Internet Activity
Do you like American food? Go to **Berlitz Hotspot** for links to some restaurants. Look at the sites and practice [practise] ordering some dishes that sound interesting to you.

Video 3 – Are You Ready to Order?
A man orders food at a restaurant. What does the waitress ask him? How does he respond? Watch the video and learn how to place a food and drink order.

Lesson 5

Would You Like Some Water?

LESSON OBJECTIVES

Lesson 5 is about offering food and drink.
When you finish this lesson, you'll know how to:

- offer someone food or drink
- offer someone choices

DIALOGUE

 Listen to the salesclerk [sales assistant] at a supermarket offer samples of food and drink.

Clerk: **Good morning. Would you like some cheese?**

Customer 1: **Sure, thank you.**

Clerk: **Sir, would you like some, too?**

Customer 2: **OK, thanks.**

Clerk: **You're welcome.**

Customer 3: **What's this?**

Clerk: **It's potato salad. Would you like some?**

Customer 3: **Yes, please. Mmm, it's good! And what's that? Is that potato salad, too?**

Clerk: **No, it's onion dip. Would you like some?**

Customer 3: **Sure, thank you. Mmm. How much is it?**

1. DIALOGUE ACTIVITY

What items does the clerk [assistant] offer the customers to try?

cheese

Which items do the customers say that they like?

potato salad

Use the following words and expressions to
guide you through the lesson.

apple	onion dip
bean dip	or
cheese	potato salad
chips [crisps]	salsa
cracker	snack
cream	some
(a) drink	sure
drink, to	too
ginger ale	What?
good (tasty)	white
How about...?	wine
man	woman
No, thanks.	You're welcome.

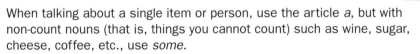

Some + Non-count Nouns

GRAMMAR

When talking about a single item or person, use the article *a*, but with
non-count nouns (that is, things you cannot count) such as wine, sugar,
cheese, coffee, etc., use *some*.

Would you like some wine?

How about a sandwich or some potato salad?

I'll have some coffee.

Some can also be used as a pronoun:

The cheese is good. Would you like some?

2. LISTENING ACTIVITY

 Listen to the host at a party offer his guests something to eat and drink. Write D (David) or J (Jane) next to the items each person eats or drinks.

white wine	J
ginger ale	
cheese and crackers	
onion dip	

Host: Oh, David, hi!

David: Hello!

Host: David, this is Jane.

David: Hi, Jane. Nice to meet you.

Jane: Hello.

Host: Would you like a drink? Wine? Ginger ale? Juice?

Jane: Oh, I'd like white wine, please.

Host: David, how about you? White wine?

David: No, thanks. I'll have ginger ale.

Host: Here you are. David, how about some cheese and crackers?

David: Sure. Thanks.

Host: Jane, would you like some cheese and crackers?

Jane: I'm fine, thanks. What's this?

Host: It's onion dip. Would you like some?

Jane: Thanks. Mmm, it's good!

3. LISTENING ACTIVITY

Listen to the host talk to another one of his guests. Fill in the missing words.

Host: **Carol,** | would | | | | **salsa and**

chips [crisps]?

Carol: | | **, thanks.** | | **?**

Host: | **bean dip.** | **you** | | **?**

Carol: | **. Mmm,** | **good!**

4. SPEAKING ACTIVITY

Imagine you are on a flight from New York to London. Complete this conversation with the flight attendant.

Flight attendant: **Would you like something to drink?**

You: Tell her you'd like some coffee.

Flight attendant: **Cream and sugar?**

You: Tell her you'd like cream.

Flight attendant: **Would you like a snack?**

You: Refuse politely.

5. SPEAKING ACTIVITY

Imagine you have invited a few friends over to your house. Offer your guests something to eat and drink.

DID YOU KNOW?

Potato *chips* are called *crisps* in Britain. The word *chips* is used for deep-fried *chipped* potatoes, called *French fries* in North America.

The words *this* and *that* are demonstratives. They are used to point, figuratively, to something. *This* points to an item that is near: physically or figuratively. *That* signals something that is far. Both can be used as pronouns and as adjectives.

Adjective

Excuse me, how much   That furniture is
is this French wine?   beautiful.

Pronoun

Oh, is this your wine? Sorry!

That isn't Jane's car.

What's that?

6. SPEAKING ACTIVITY

A guest you invited over to your house is very difficult to please. Offer him/her the following items, using *some* and *a/an*.

1. **apple**   ***Would you like an apple?***

2. **cheese and crackers**

3. **chips [crisps]**

4. **ginger ale**

5. **salad**

7. WRITING ACTIVITY

Use *or* and *this/that*, following the example.

Example: Would you like some salad? This potato salad or that green salad?

1. **dip: onion dip/bean dip**

2. **soda: ginger ale/cola**

3. **hot drink: coffee/tea**

4. **wine: white wine/red wine**

8. READING ACTIVITY

Complete the following dialogue. Use *this/that* or *some*.

Jane: **Excuse me. Is** | this | **your wine?**

David: **No,** | | **isn't my wine.** | | **is**

my wine.

Jane: **Oh, sorry! I thought** | | **was my wine.**

David: **No, no. It's my wine.**

Jane: **You don't have much. Would you like** | | **more?**

David: **Sure! I'll have** | | **more. Thanks.**

Check It!

Test what you've learned in this lesson and review anything you're not sure of.

CAN YOU . . . ?

☐ **offer someone food and drink**
Would you like some cheese?
How about some chips [crisps]?

☐ **use *some* with non-count nouns**
Would you like some wine?
How about a sandwich or some potato salad?

☐ **use *this/that* as an adjective**
Excuse me, how much is this French wine?
That car is Japanese.

☐ **use *this/that* as a pronoun:**
Oh, is this your wine? Sorry!
That isn't Jane's car.
What's that?

☐ **offer choices**
Would you like some salad? This potato salad or that green salad?

 BERLITZ HOTSPOT Go to www.berlitzhotspot.com for...

Social Networking
Chat with your Hotspot friends about the food you've tried from English-speaking countries, or would like to try. Ask them about their food and drink preferences.

 Podcast 5
Some vs. Any
Download this podcast.

 Internet Activity
Go to **Berlitz Hotspot** for links for the menus of popular American restaurants. Practice [practise] offering the food items. Be sure to use *some* or *this/that* as needed!

Lesson 6

Do You Have Postcards?

LESSON OBJECTIVES

Lesson 6 is about buying things. When you finish this lesson, you'll know how to:

- understand an offer of help in a shop
- ask for what you want to buy in a shop
- describe items

DIALOGUE

Listen to these people shopping in a store.

1.

Customer 1:	**Excuse me. Do you have any postcards?**
Salesclerk:	**Yes, we do. They're here.**
Customer 1:	**Oh, yes. How much are they, please?**
Salesclerk:	**Eighty-five pence.**
Customer 1:	**OK. I'll take three.**

2.

Customer 2:	**Excuse me.**
Salesclerk:	**Yes?**
Customer 2:	**How much is that camera?**
Salesclerk:	**It's a hundred and fifty pounds.**
Customer 2:	**Mmm. Could I see it, please?**
Salesclerk:	**Of course. Here you are.**
Customer 2:	**It's nice.**

3.

Customer 3:	**Excuse me. Do you have any maps?**
Salesclerk:	**Yes. The maps are over there.**
Customer 3:	**Oh yes. How much are they, please?**
Salesclerk:	**Seven ninety-nine.**

1. DIALOGUE ACTIVITY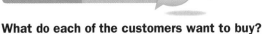

What do each of the customers want to buy?

postcards		

How much does each item cost?

85p		

Use the following words and expressions to
guide you through the lesson.

VOCABULARY

Anything else?	**memory card** (for a digital camera)
bad	**new**
bag	**newspaper**
beautiful	**nice**
big	**not bad**
book	**of course**
camera	**old**
candy bar [chocolate bar]	**only**
cheap	**over there**
color(s) [colour(s)]	**pen**
Could I see it, please?	**postcard**
Do you have any...?	**to see**
expensive	**small**
glass	**T-shirt**
to have	**them**
How much do the items cost?	**these**
idea	**those**
I'll take...	**very**
inexpensive	**watch**
interesting	**well...**
Let me see.	**Yes, we do.**
map	

COLORS [COLOURS]

black	**pink**
blue	**purple**
brown	**red**
gray [grey]	**white**
green	**yellow**
orange	

2. LISTENING ACTIVITY

Listen to two other people buy things. Write the number of the customer next to the items they would like to buy. Then write the price of each item on the tag.

1.

Customer:	Excuse me. How much is that bag?
Salesclerk:	The black bag? It's fifteen dollars.
Customer:	It's nice. Yes, I'll take it.
Salesclerk:	Thank you.

a bag

2.

Customer:	Excuse me. How much are the candy [chocolate] bars?
Salesclerk:	Seventy-five cents.
Customer:	OK, I'll take two, please.
Salesclerk:	Anything else?
Customer:	Yes. Do you have any maps of New York?
Salesclerk:	Maps? Yes, here they are. How about these?
Customer:	Hmm, they're very small. How much are they?
Salesclerk:	Three fifty.
Customer:	Hmm, no thank you.

3. READING ACTIVITY

Match each phrase with the best answer.

1. How much is this book?
2. Can I help you?
3. Thank you.
4. Do you have any maps?
5. How about this watch?

a. You're welcome.
b. It's very nice.
c. Sure. Here they are.
d. It's $15.99.
e. Yes, please. Could I see that book?

60

4. LISTENING ACTIVITY

Listen to some people shop for a gift for a friend. Then look at the adjectives below. Check (✔) the ones you hear.

expensive		cheap		nice	✔
big		good		beautiful	
new		old		interesting	
small		inexpensive			

Man 1:	**This is a nice book.**
Woman 1:	**Yes, it is. How much is it?**
Man 1:	**Let me see. Sixty-five dollars!**
Woman 1:	**Sixty-five dollars! That's expensive.**
Man 1:	**How about those T-shirts?**
Woman 1:	**Hmm, they're interesting colors [colours]. Excuse me. Can I see those blue and green T-shirts?**
Salesclerk:	**Here you are.**
Woman 1:	**Thank you. Oh, they're very big. Do you have any small T-shirts?**
Salesclerk:	**No, I'm sorry. Only these.**
Woman 1:	**Oh.**
Man 1:	**How about some wine glasses?**
Woman 1:	**No.**
Man 1:	**How about a bag? A new bag?**
Woman 1:	**That's a good idea! Look. Those are nice.**
Man 1:	**Hmm. Excuse me. Could we see that black bag?**

LEARNING TIP

Keep a notebook of words you have learned and review it in your free time.

Plural Nouns

To form the plural of nouns, add -s to the end of the word:

Their names are Susan and Tom.

The red T-shirts are nice!

Add -es to words that end in the following: -s, -z, -ch.

The sandwiches are cheap.

Where are the wine glasses?

Add -ies to words that end in a consonant + -y:

The pastries are expensive.

Memorize any irregular forms, such as *man/men, woman/women, child/children*.

The men are French, and the women are German.

---

5. SPEAKING ACTIVITY

Look at the items below. Describe each one.

Example: 1. It's a red bag/That's a red bag.

GRAMMAR

These/Those

The plural forms of *this/that* are *these/those*.

These aren't tuna sandwiches!

Excuse me, how much are these shirts?

Those cups are from China.

6. WRITING ACTIVITY

Change the following singular nouns to the plural. Then read your answers aloud.

1.	**apple**	apples	6.	**map**	
2.	**pastry**		7.	**postcard**	
3.	**camera**		8.	**telephone**	
4.	**sandwich**		9.	**watch**	
5.	**man**		10.	**pencil**	

GRAMMAR

In English, adjectives usually come before the word they describe.

Do you have any cheap cameras?

Two black T-shirts, please.

7.  WRITING ACTIVITY

Change *this/that* in the following sentences to *these/those*. Make any other changes to make the sentence correct.

1. **How much is that bag?**

   > **How much are those bags?**

2. **This isn't a blue T-shirt, it's a black T-shirt.**

3. **That camera isn't expensive.**

4. **This watch is too big.**

5. **That is a very nice book.**

6. **This cellphone [mobile phone] is expensive.**

PRONUNCIATION

1. In English, the final -s is pronounced in three different ways.

/s/	/z/	/ɪz/
books	pens	watches
cups	cars	oranges

2. Listen to the audio and practice [practise] these words.

maps	newspapers	watches
sandwiches	postcards	cameras

8. SPEAKING ACTIVITY

What would you say in the following situations? Write down your answer and then say it aloud.

1. **You're at a newsstand. You want to know if they have any Spanish newspapers.**

   Excuse me, do you have any Spanish newspapers?

2. **You see a small camera you like. You want to know how much it costs.**

3. **You see a pen you like. You want the salesperson to show it to you.**

4. **You want to buy a cheap camera. Get the salesperson's attention.**

5. **A salesperson is showing you some T-shirts. You want to know if there are any red ones.**

Check It!

Test what you learned in this lesson. Review anything you're not sure of.

CAN YOU . . . ?

☐ **ask for an item in a store**
Excuse me. Do you have any postcards?
Could we see that black bag?

☐ **ask how much something costs**
How much are they, please?
How much is that camera?

☐ **name the basic colors [colours]**
black, blue, brown, gray [grey], green...

☐ **describe items**
This is a nice book.
Do you have any small T-shirts?

☐ **make singular nouns plural**
watch   watches
pastry   pastries

☐ **use *these/those* properly**
These aren't tuna sandwiches!
Excuse me, how much are those?

☐ **place adjectives before the word they are describing**
Do you have any cheap cameras?
Two black T-shirts, please.

☐ **say the final *-s* in a plural correctly**
books   pens   watches

Learn More

Make a list of American and British souvenirs in English. Use your dictionary to look up the items you don't know. Practice [Practise] asking for the things in different colors and amounts.

 BERLITZ HOTSPOT   Go to www.berlitzhotspot.com for...

Social Networking
Go to **Berlitz Hotspot** and share your thoughts about what you're learning. If you've traveled [travelled] to English-speaking countries, share information about stores you visited with your Hotspot friends.

 Podcast 6
Where to Shop?
Download this podcast.

 Internet Activity
Search for some large American and British stores on the internet and look at their current catalogues. See how many items you can identify.

 Video 4 – The Souvenir Shop
A woman makes a purchase at a souvenir shop. What does she ask the salesclerk [sales assistant]? How much do the items cost? Watch the video and learn how to find and buy items in a store.

Lesson 7

What Do You Do?

DIALOGUE

 Listen to this conversation between people eating in the park during their lunch hour.

> Hi! Well, my name's Susan and I work in that department store over there, the large brown building. I'm a salesclerk [sales assistant]. This is my friend Jane.

> Hi, I'm Jane. I work in the department store, too, but I'm a secretary. I work in the personnel office in the store.

> My name's Tom and I'm a teacher, a school teacher. I teach French in a high school [secondary school]. It isn't very easy.

> My name's David, David Short, and I'm an accountant. It's, uh, yes, it's interesting.

1. DIALOGUE ACTIVITY

What are some of the jobs mentioned?

salesclerk [sales assistant]	

What are some of the things people say about the jobs?

It isn't very easy.	

68

Use the following words and expressions to
guide you through the lesson.

VOCABULARY

at	nationality
bank	occupation
building	office
but	personnel
by the way	Really?
company	restaurant
computer	retired
department store	school
to do	store
easy	to teach
employer	theater [theatre]
engineering	unemployed
high school [secondary school]	university
hospital	What do you do?
hotel	wife
in	to work (for)
job	young
large	

OCCUPATIONS

accountant	salesclerk [sales assistant]
actor (male), actress (female)	salesman
doctor	secretary
housewife	student
journalist	teacher
nurse	waiter (male), waitress (female)

2. LISTENING ACTIVITY

 Listen to these people meeting for the first time at a party. They are asking each other about what they do. Write each person's name under his or her photo.

Jane

Steve:	**Would you like some wine?**
Jane:	**Oh, yes, thanks.**
Steve:	**By the way, I'm Steve Woods.**
Jane:	**Nice to meet you. I'm Jane Bond.**
Steve:	**So, what do you do, Jane? Do you work in New York?**
Jane:	**Yes, I'm a teacher.**
Steve:	**Yeah? What do you teach?**
Jane:	**I teach Spanish in a high school [secondary school].** **How about you, Steve? What do you do?**
Steve:	**I work for a computer company.**
Jane:	**Is it interesting?**
Steve:	**Yes, it is.**

Robert: **What do you do, Linda?**

Linda: **I'm a journalist, for ABC News.**

Robert: **A journalist!**

Linda: **Yes. How about you? What do you do, Robert?**

Robert: **I'm unemployed. I'm an actor, but my wife Judy works.
Judy's a nurse at City Hospital.**

3. WRITING ACTIVITY

Fill in the missing information, then listen to the first conversation in Activity 2
again to check your answers.

Steve: **So, what** ___do___ ___you___

___do___ **, Jane?** ___ **you**

___ **in New York?**

Jane: **Yes,** ___ **a teacher.**

Steve: **Yeah? What** ___ **you** ___ **?**

Jane: **I teach Spanish** ___ **a high** ___ **.**

How ___ **you, Steve? What** ___

___ **do?**

Steve: ___ ___ **for a computer company.**

Jane: ___ ___ **interesting?**

Steve: **Yes,** ___ ___ **.**

4. WRITING ACTIVITY

Match the occupation to the workplace.

A/An...	works....
teacher	in a hospital
secretary	in a theater [theatre]
salesclerk [sales assistant]	in a school
nurse	in an office
waiter	in a department store
journalist	in a newspaper office
actor	in a restaurant

5. WRITING ACTIVITY

Complete the questions below with *is/are* or *do/does*. Then write short responses using the words in parentheses.

1. **Do** you work in a large store?

   (no, small) No, I work in a small store.

2. _____ Mr. Woods work for Delta Engineering?

   (yes) _____

3. _____ Jack and John students?

   (yes) _____

4. _____ Mrs. Garcia teach in a high school [secondary school]?

   (no, university) _____

5. _____ Steve a computer salesman?

   (no, car salesman) _____

6. _____ Mr. and Mrs. Massey both work in Paris?

   (yes) _____

6. WRITING ACTIVITY

 Listen to two friends talk about a new neighbor [neighbour]. Write the details on her ID card.

Man 1:	**So, is she old?**
Man 2:	**No, she isn't old. She's young.**
Man 1:	**What's her name?**
Man 2:	**Her name's Sylvia Dupont.**
Man 1:	**Sylvia. Hmm. Nice name. Where's she from?**
Man 2:	**She's from Paris.**
Man 1:	**She's French? What does she do?**
Man 2:	**She's a doctor.**
Man 1:	**Really? Where does she work?**
Man 2:	**She works at City Hospital.**

➕ CITY HOSPITAL

Name: Sylvia Dupont
Nationality: _____
Occupation: _____
Employer: _____

7. WRITING ACTIVITY

You have a new neighbor [neighbour], David Forest, and a friend of yours asks about him. Answer the questions with the information from David's card.

ONN

Name: David Forest
Nationality: Canadian
Occupation: Journalist
Employer: ONN

Friend: **What's his name?**

You:

Friend: **Where's he from?**

You:

Friend: **What does he do?**

You:

Friend: **Where does he work?**

You:

Simple Present Tense

We use the present tense to talk about general situations or actions.

Affirmative Form

The third person singular (he/she/it) adds *-s* or *-es* to the end of the verb. The other forms (I, you, we, they) are like the infinitive without *to*.

> I work for a car company, and David teaches English.
>
> She works in a department store.

Note that the verb *to have* is irregular: He/She/It has.

> I have a good job, but she has a good job, too.
>
> They have a new car.

Negative Form

> I/you/they + do not + verb   he/she/it + does not + verb

In spoken English, these forms are usually contracted to: *don't, doesn't.*

> I don't work for a car company. = I do not work for a car company.
>
> She doesn't teach French. = She does not teach French.
>
> The hotel doesn't have a nice restaurant.
>
> They don't have a new car.

Interrogative Form of to Do

Do you work for a car company?

Does she teach French?

Does the hotel have a nice restaurant?

Short Answers

Yes, I/you/we/they do.	Yes, he/she/it does.
No, I/you/we/they don't.	No, he/she doesn't.

Does she work in New York?	Yes, she does.
Do Mr. and Mrs. Johnson have a new car?	No, they don't.
Does she have any children?	No, she doesn't.

8. WRITING ACTIVITY

Pretend you are at a party. Introduce yourself to someone new. Give five simple sentences in the present tense about yourself. Talk about where you are from, what you do, etc.

1. **Hello! My name is Dominika. I'm from Poland. I'm a journalist.**

2.

3.

4.

5.

6.

9. SPEAKING ACTIVITY

Pablo just moved to your town. Ask a neighbor [neighbour] questions about Pablo, using *do*, *what*, *where*, etc. Give the neighbor's [neighbour's] responses as short answers.

1. **Question**   **Does Pablo have any children?**

   Answer

2. **Question**

   Answer

3. **Question**

   Answer

Check It!

Test what you learned in this lesson. Review anything you're not sure of.

CAN YOU . . . ?

☐ **say your profession**
I'm a salesclerk [sales assistant].
I'm a teacher.

☐ **name some occupations**
accountant
actor [male], actress [female]
doctor
housewife
journalist

☐ **name the places where people work**
A teacher works in a school.
A nurse works in a hospital.

☐ **ask questions about people**
What's his name?
Where's he from?
What does he do?

☐ **give answers in the affirmative and in the negative**
I work in a hospital./I don't work in a hospital.
I teach French./She doesn't teach French.

☐ **ask questions using** *do*
Does she teach French?
Does the hotel have a nice restaurant?

☐ **give short answers to questions**
Does she work in New York?
Yes, she does.
Do Mr. and Mrs. Johnson have a new car?
No, they don't.

 BERLITZ HOTSPOT Go to www.berlitzhotspot.com for...

Social Networking
Tell your Hotspot friends about you and your job. Do you like what you do?

 Podcast 7
Work, Work, Work
Download this podcast.

 Internet Activity
Search for photos of famous people on the internet. Tell a story about the people in the pictures. Say where they are from or where they live. Use the vocabulary from this section. Try to use vocabulary from previous sections.

Lesson 8

This Is My Family.

LESSON OBJECTIVES

Lesson 8 is about family. When you finish this lesson, you'll know how to:

- talk about relationships
- describe your family
- give information about your family members

DIALOGUE

Listen to the conversation between two people as they look at some family photos.

Woman: **Who's that? He's nice.**

Man: **That's my brother. His name's Bob.**

Woman: **Really? What does your brother do?**

Man: **He's an engineer. He works for Benson's.**

Woman: **Mmm. Is he married?**

Man: **Separated.**

Woman: **Separated, eh? Does he work here in London?**

Man: **No, he works in Glasgow.**

Woman: **Oh…And who's that?**

Man: **That's his friend, Tony. He works for Benson's, too, but he works in the Cardiff office.**

Woman: **And the little girl? Who's she?**

Man: **That's Tony's daughter. My brother Bob has a young son, but he and his mother are in France.**

1. DIALOGUE ACTIVITY

Who are the people in the picture with Bob?

Tony

What is their relationship to Bob?

Use the following words and expressions to guide you through the lesson.

VOCABULARY

any	How old is/are...?
baby	husband
boy	married
boyfriend	mother
brother	parents
children	partner
daughter	separated
divorced	single
engineer	sister
father	son
friend	too
girl	Who?
girlfriend	widower (male)/widow (female)

2. LISTENING ACTIVITY

 Listen to the conversation about Bob again and check (✔) the correct answers.

1.	Bob's	a teacher.		an engineer.	✔	unemployed.	
2.	He's	separated.		single.		divorced.	
3.	He works	in Glasgow.		in London.		for Benson's.	
4.	Tony is Bob's	brother.		son.		friend.	
5.	Bob	has a son.		has a daughter.		doesn't have any children.	

79

3. WRITING ACTIVITY

Put the words in the correct order to form questions; be sure to capitalize the first letter of the first word. Then match each question with an appropriate answer.

1. your/does/work/husband?

   > Does your husband work?

   a. Ten and six.

2. brothers'/your/what/names/are?

   b. German.

3. sister/children/does/have/your/any?

   c. No, he doesn't.

4. do/live/parents/where/your?

   d. Yes, she has two.

5. children/how/are/old/your?

   e. Bob and Tom.

6. does/what/wife/teach/his?

   f. In San Francisco.

GRAMMAR

When a word is plural and ends in -s, possession is shown by adding an apostrophe (').

My brothers' names are Michael and James.

The girls' books are on the table.

4. LISTENING ACTIVITY

Listen to David and Jane talk about their families. Fill in the information in the table below.

	David	Jane
number of children	2	5
number of boys		
ages of boys		
number of girls		
ages of girls		

Jane: **So, do you have any children, David?**

David: **Yes, I have two sons.**

Jane: **And how old are they?**

David: **Steven is nine, and Paul is fourteen. How about you, Jane? Do you have any children?**

Jane: **Yes, I have five.**

David: **Five children! Are they boys or girls?**

Jane: **Two boys and three girls.**

David: **And how old are they?**

Jane: **The boys are three and seven, and the girls are five, nine, and thirteen.**

David: **Five children...**

GRAMMAR

Note that *a/any* are usually not translated into other languages when forming questions.

When you ask about one object or person, use *a*.

> Do you have a car?
>
> Does your son have a girlfriend?

When you ask about more than one object or person, use *any*.

> Do they have any children?
>
> Do you teach any Japanese students?

Also use *any* in negative sentences.

> I don't have any children.
>
> The school doesn't have any computers.

But:

> We don't have a car.

Prepositions

In is used to show a location.

> Jane works in a bank.
>
> Is the company in London?

For or *at* comes before the name of a company or a specific organization.

> Do you teach at the university?
>
> My wife is a nurse at City Hospital.
>
> I work for a computer company in New York.

5. SPEAKING ACTIVITY

 What information can you give about yourself, a member of your family or a friend? First listen to the example, then you try. Here are some hints:

- **name**
- **age**
- **job**
- **employer**
- **where**
- **family: brother or sister, children**

Who's this?

This is my big sister. Her name's Laura and she's a secretary in a big company. Um, she's twenty-one years old and she's married. And her husband's name is Tony. And, um, oh yes! And she has a baby. And her baby's name is Tony, too.

6. WRITING ACTIVITY

Add *a/any* to the following sentences.

1. **Do you have**   a   **brother?**

2. **She doesn't have** _____ **children.**

3. **She will have** _____ **baby boy.**

4. **Do you have** _____ **daughters?**

5. **Do you have** _____ **married friends?**

6. **Does he have** _____ **girlfriend? Or is he single?**

7. SPEAKING ACTIVITY 66 99

Say where you work or study and in which town your job or school are located. Then do the same for your family members and close friends.

Example: I work at a school in Los Angeles. Or, I work for School Number 13 in Los Angeles.

8. WRITING ACTIVITY

Draw a simple family tree and explain each person's relationship to you.

9. SPEAKING ACTIVITY 66 99

Find a photo of your family. Describe the photo and give information about each person.

10. WRITING ACTIVITY

Read the following text by Lucy about her life and work. Then write a similar text about your life.

My name is Lucy, and I am 28 years old. I have a boyfriend, and we plan to get married in a year or two. I have no children, and all of my family lives very far away. I have two sisters and a brother. My sisters are named Lizzy and Laura, and my brother is named Tim. My sisters and brother are younger than I am. I am English, but I work in New York. I am a nurse and work at a big hospital in Manhattan.

Check It!

Test what you learned in this lesson. Review anything you're not sure of.

CAN YOU . . . ?

☐ **describe people's relationships**
That's his friend, Tony.
That's Tony's daughter.

☐ **describe your family**
I have two sons.
I have five children.

☐ **give information about your family members**
Bob's separated.
My sister's husband's name is Tony.

☐ **use *a* and *any***
Do you have a car?
Do they have any children?

☐ **use *in* to show a location**
Jane works in a bank.
Is the company in London?

☐ **use *for* or *at* before the name of a company or a specific organization**
Do you teach at the university?
My wife is a nurse at City Hospital.

BERLITZ HOTSPOT   Go to www.berlitzhotspot.com for...

Social Networking
Tell your Hotspot friends about your family.

Podcast 8
An English-Speaking Wedding
Download this podcast.

Internet Activity
Search for photos of families or groups of people on the internet. Make up stories for each photo and describe the people that you see. Use the vocabulary and grammar you have learned so far.

Video 5 – My Family
Two friends talk about family relationships. How many siblings, or brothers and sisters, does the man have? Who's married? Watch the video and learn how to talk about your family.

Lesson 9

Where Do You Live?

LESSON OBJECTIVES

Lesson 9 is about where people live. When you finish this lesson, you'll know how to:

- describe where you live
- describe the furniture in a room

DIALOGUE

 Listen to some British people talk about where they live.

1.

Interviewer: **Where do you live?**

Woman 1: **We live in Manchester.**

Interviewer: **In a flat?**

Woman 1: **Yes, we have a small flat.**

2.

Interviewer: **Excuse me. Where do you live?**

Woman 2: **In London.**

Interviewer: **In the city?**

Woman 2: **No, in the suburbs. I have a small house in Greenwich.**

3.

Interviewer: **And where do you live?**

Woman 3: **In Scotland. In a little cottage.**

4.

Interviewer: **Where do you live?**

Woman 4: **My husband and I live in Paris. We have an apartment [flat] in the suburbs.**

1. DIALOGUE ACTIVITY

What were some of the places you heard?

Manchester			

What were some of the different types of places to live?

Use the following words and expressions to guide you through the lesson.

VOCABULARY

address

age

apartment [flat]

Arabic

bathroom

bed

bedroom

carpet

chair

Chinese

city

cottage

couch [sofa]

desk

dining room

fireplace

floor

furniture

garden

German

house

Japanese

to know

kitchen

Korean

a little

to live

living room

marital status (single, married, divorced, widowed)

more

news

not very well

parquet

Polish

Portuguese

really (very)

rent

Russian

to speak

still

suburbs

table

TV/television

week

window

2. LISTENING ACTIVITY

Listen to three people talk about where their family members live. Complete the following sentences. Then listen again to check your answer.

1. **My parents** [have] **a small** [＿＿] **in** [＿＿] [＿＿] .

2. **My daughter and her husband** [＿＿] [＿＿] [＿＿] **beautiful** [＿＿] [＿＿] [＿＿] **suburbs.**

3. **My** [＿＿] **in is in a large** [＿＿] [＿＿] **in the** [＿＿] .

> I live here, but my parents live in Boston. They have a small apartment [flat] in the city. The building is old, and it's small, but it's really nice.

> My daughter's married, and she lives in London. She and her husband have a beautiful house in the suburbs. A beautiful big house. And they have a large garden, too.

> I live in Los Angeles. My apartment's [flat] in a large new building in the suburbs. It's really nice.

3. WRITING ACTIVITY

This is a letter that Steven Black received from some friends. Complete the message by choosing words or phrases from the box below.

new house	new baby	live in	study	are you
the suburbs	How about	large garden	work for	children

3645 Oakhill Drive | Sacramento, CA 95831 | Tel: 916-395-1515

Hi, how **are you** ? We're fine. Did you see — we have a _____ ! It's not very big, but it's in _____ , and it has a _____ . And we have some more news — we have a _____ ! Her name's Marie, and she's ten weeks old, she's beautiful. So now we have three _____ .

_____ you? Do you still _____ that engineering company? Do you still have that nice girlfriend? Does your mother still _____ Rio? Do you still _____ Portuguese? Call us, please!

Bye,

Angie and Ted

Good or Well?

Good is an adjective (an adjective describes a noun). *Well* is an adverb (an adverb describes a verb).

He speaks good Chinese.	He speaks Chinese well.
Your Polish is good.	You speak it well.
She's a good teacher.	She teaches well.

Object Pronouns

These pronouns are used when they are the object of the verb. They receive the action of the verb.

He speaks Spanish and Italian, and he speaks them very well.

Where do you teach English? I teach it at the university.

Do you know Susan? Yes, but I don't know her very well.

Subject	Object
I	me
you	you
he	him
she	her
it	it
we	us
you	you
they	them

4. WRITING ACTIVITY

Answer the following questions. Use the word or words in parentheses.

1. **Do you know Amy? (yes)**

   Yes, I know her.

2. **Where do you teach Arabic? (high school [secondary school])**

3. **Do you have the green bag? (no)**

4. **Do you know Phil and Ted? (yes)**

5. **Do your parents still have an apartment [flat] in Paris? (yes)**

6. **Do you want the TV on or off? (off)**

7. **Where should we put our bags? (living room)**

8. **Do you speak Korean? (yes, well)**

5. READING ACTIVITY

Two friends who haven't seen each other for a long time connect over the internet. Read their conversation. Circle where Jane lives and where she works.

SEND DELETE

To:
From:
Subject:

Dear Jane,

I am so happy that I saw your mother the other day. She gave me your new e-mail address! How are you doing? I haven't seen you in such a long time. Where do you live? What do you do? I have so many questions!

Natalie

>Jane's Reply:

Dear Natalie,

I am so happy to hear from you after all these years! How are you? I am doing well. I live in London now and I work for a newspaper. I love being in the city and there is so much to do. The rent here is expensive, so I live in a small apartment [flat] that I share with a friend. We have two bedrooms, a bathroom, a living room, a kitchen and a small area where we have the table. I don't think I'd call it a dining room! But, I like it.

I remember you were learning Japanese. Well, in my spare time I have been giving English lessons to Japanese speakers. I don't speak Japanese very well yet, but their English is getting pretty good!

I have lots of questions for you, too! What have you been doing lately?

Question Intonation

PRONUNCIATION

Questions that can be answered *yes* or *no* usually have a rising intonation. Questions that begin with a question word such as *where*, *what* and *how* usually have a falling intonation.

Do you live in a house?

Where do you live?

6. WRITING ACTIVITY

Imagine you receive a message from an old friend similar to Natalie's message. Greet your friend. Tell him or her a bit about where you live and where you work.

```
■ ■ ■                                                    ✉

✉ SEND    ✖ DELETE

    To: [                                    ]
  From: [                                    ]
Subject: [                                   ]

```

7. LISTENING ACTIVITY

 Listen to the following questions. Notice how the speakers use rising intonation for *yes/no* questions and falling intonation for questions that begin with a question word.

Rising intonation

1. **Is she married?**

2. **Does she speak French?**

3. **Do they live in London?**

Falling intonation

4. **Where does she live?**

5. **How old is your brother?**

6. **What do you do?**

8. SPEAKING ACTIVITY

 Read the questions aloud with the correct intonation. Do they have rising or falling intonation? Then listen to check your answers.

1. **Where does she live?**

2. **Does she teach Spanish?**

3. **How old is he?**

4. **Does your son work in New York?**

5. **Are you American?**

6. **What does he do?**

9. SPEAKING ACTIVITY "

Read the questions aloud. Then answer them with information about yourself. Use the vocabulary and grammar you have learned so far. Prepare your answers by writing them down.

1. **Where do you live?**

2. **Do you live in a house or an apartment [a flat]?**

3. **Is it big or small?**

4. **How many bedrooms does it have?**

5. **Whom do you live with?**

6. **What furniture do you have in your living room?**

7. **Where do you work/study?**

8. **What do you do?**

9. **Which languages do you speak?**

10. **Do you speak them well?**

Check It!

Test what you learned in this lesson. Review anything you're not sure of.

CAN YOU . . . ?

☐ **say where you live**
We live in Manchester.
We live in London.

☐ **say the type of housing you live in**
We have a small apartment [flat].
We have a large house in the suburbs.

☐ **describe the rooms your house/ apartment [flat] has**
My apartment [flat] has two bedrooms.
It has a small kitchen and a living room.

☐ **describe the furniture in your home**
We have a couch [sofa], a small table and two chairs.
My apartment [flat] has a fireplace.

☐ **use *good* and *well* appropriately**

He speaks good German.	He speaks German well.
Your English is good.	You speak it well.

☐ **use object pronouns**
He speaks Spanish and Italian, and he speaks *them* very well.
Do you know Susan? Yes, but I don't know *her* very well.

☐ **use the appropriate intonation for questions**
yes/no: rising intonation
question word: falling intonation.

Learn More

Read the employment advertisement in an online English-language newspaper to see how many of the jobs you recognize. Use clues such a the name of the company. Guess wh the job title means, and then check your dictionary.

 BERLITZ HOTSPOT Go to www.berlitzhotspot.com for...

 Social Networking
Where do you live? In a house? In an apartment [a flat]? Is it typical for the area that you live in? Tell your Hotspot friends about it.

 Podcast 9
All Types of Housing
Download this podcast

 Internet Activity
Go to **Berlitz Hotspot** for a list of websites for real estate agencies. Do some quick searches for places to live that are now available. Describe the different types of places and the way the rooms are furnished in the images.

Test 1 — Review of Lessons 1–9

1. Which word is different from the others in the group?

1. Japanese	Spanish	<u>England</u>	French	Italian
2. seven	ninth	eight	three	two
3. iced tea	lemon	coffee	juice	cola
4. interesting	expensive	beautiful	only	bad
5. postcard	camera	those	book	map
6. hot dog	hamburger	water	omelet [omelette]	pastry

2. Choose the most appropriate answers.

1. **What time is it in Tokyo?**
   a. **Wednesday.**   b. **It's morning.**   c. <u>**Four o'clock.**</u>

2. **How are you?**
   a. **Sorry.**   b. **Fine.**   c. **Hello.**

3. **Is your car Japanese?**
   a. **Yes, it is.**   b. **Yes, I have.**   c. **No, they aren't.**

4. **What would you like?**
   a. **Oh, good.**   b. **No, thanks.**   c. **A hamburger, please.**

5. **Do you have any postcards?**
   a. **Yes, we do.**   b. **Yes, they do.**   c. **No, he doesn't.**

6. **Are we late?**
   a. **No, I'm not.**   b. **Yes, we are.**   c. **You're welcome.**

3. Put the sentences in order to create a dialogue. The first one is done for you.

1.   **£200? Oh, that's very expensive! Do you have any cheap cameras?**

2.   **Can I help you?**

3.   **That's pretty good. I'll take it.**

4.   **That camera? It's £200.**

5.   **Yes, please. How much is that digital camera?**

6.   **You're welcome.**

7.   **...and your receipt.**

8.   **Let me see...yes. This camera is £70.**

9.   **Here you are. Your camera...**

10. **Thank you.**

Salesperson: Can I help you?

4. Rearrange the words to form complete sentences.

1. **in / time / is / what / it / Rome?**

   > What time is it in Rome?

2. **does / green / cost / what / the / salad?**

3. **newspapers / are / China / those / from?**

4. **have / tea / I'll / some?**

5. **any / soda / do / have / you?**

6. **something / would / to / you / drink / like?**

5. Fill in the blank with the correct word.

1. The men are French and the 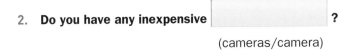 is Japanese.

    (woman/women)

2. Do you have any inexpensive 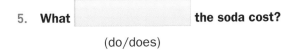 ?

    (cameras/camera)

3. How much are  maps?

    (this/these)

4. 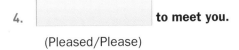 to meet you.

    (Pleased/Please)

5. What  the soda cost?

    (do/does)

6. It's nine o'clock  night in Madrid.

    (in/at)

6. The following are responses to a series of questions. Write the appropriate questions.

1.
> **What would you like to drink?**

I'll have ginger ale, please.

2.
>

Oh, I'd like white wine, please.

3.
>

This is onion dip. Would you like some?

4.
>

Cream, please. No sugar.

5.
>

I'll have some chips [crisps] and dip. I don't like cheese and crackers.

6.
>

I'll have some of that cheese, please.

7.
>

Sure, I'll have some salad. Thanks.

8.
>

That's bean dip. How about some with chips [crisps]?

7. Answer each question with a short answer.

1. **Are you a student?** (yes)

   Yes, I am.

2. **Is your car German?** (no)

3. **Are Judy and Jane from Boston?** (yes)

4. **Is Philip late?** (yes)

5. **Are you and Joe Canadian?** (no)

6. **Am I early?** (no)

8. Using the words given, write a sentence expressing possession.

1. **Bill/cameras**

   Bill's cameras are expensive.

2. **my/friends**

3. **Sue Fisher/team**

4. **Joe/telephone number**

5. **that woman/onion dip**

6. **Judy/car**

9. Which word is different from the others in the group?

1. six eleven five <u>second</u> twelve

2. engineer woman teacher waiter actor

3. suburbs school hotel bank store

4. easy engineer small married new

5. daughter brother friend sister son

6. coffee shop drugstore floor post office supermarket
   [chemist]

10. For each occupation, write a sentence saying where these people work.

1. secretary | A secretary works in an office.

2. doctor

3. waiter

4. teacher

5. salesclerk
   [sales assistant]

6. nurse

7. journalist

8. actor

11. Put the words in the correct order to make complete sentences.
Then give a short answer to each question.

1. **have / brothers / any / do / sisters / you / or?**

Do you have any brothers or sisters?	Yes, I do.

2. **teach / the / your / university / does / at / husband?**

3. **have / postcards / do / any / you?**

4. **at / is / your / nurse / City Hospital / wife / a**

5. **small / live / a / they / city / in / in / apartment / the**

6. **work / you / where / do**

12. Write the question for each answer.

1. **She lives in San Francisco.**

   > **Where does she live?**

2. **She's 37 years old.**

3. **Her husband's name's Steve.**

4. **She has three children.**

5. **They're nine, seven and five.**

6. **Paul works for a computer company.**

Lesson 10

The City

LESSON OBJECTIVES

Lesson 10 is about asking and giving directions.
When you finish this lesson, you'll know how to:

- get someone's attention
- ask for and give directions
- use ordinal numbers

DIALOGUE

Listen as a woman asks for directions.

Woman:	**Excuse me.**
Man 1:	**Yeah?**
Woman:	**Is there a post office near here?**
Man 1:	**Sorry, I don't know. I don't live here.**
Woman:	**Oh, I see. Sorry... Excuse me.**
Man 2:	**Yes, can I help you?**
Woman:	**Yes, please. Is there a post office near here?**
Man 2:	**Yes, there is. There's one next to the Grand Hotel.**
Woman:	**Sorry?**
Man 2:	**Do you see that Italian restaurant over there?**
Woman:	**What restaurant?**
Man 2:	**Next to the travel agency. Do you see that?**
Woman:	**Oh, on the corner?**
Man 2:	**Yes, on the corner. Well, the Grand Hotel is just around the corner, and there's a post office next to it.**
Woman:	**Thank you. Thank you very much.**
Man 2:	**You're welcome.**

Use the following words and expressions to guide you through the lesson.

VOCABULARY

across from [opposite]	near
bank	next (to)
block	over there
bus stop	park
clothes	parking lot [car park]
coffee shop	post office
computer store	pub
corner	record
drugstore [chemist]	restaurant
floor	right
gas station [petrol station]	school
here	shoe(s)
hotel	shop
in front of	supermarket
just around the corner	telephone (phone)
left	theater [theatre]
mailbox [post box]	travel agency
manager	

1. DIALOGUE ACTIVITY

Where does the woman want to go?

Which way does she need to go to get there?

2. LISTENING ACTIVITY

Listen to people ask where certain buildings are. Number the buildings on the map in the order that you hear them.

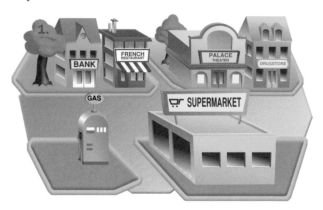

Woman 1:	**Can I help you?**
Man 1:	**Thanks. Is there a bank near here?**
Woman 1:	**Yes, there's one on the next block. It's next to a French restaurant.**
Man 1:	**Thanks.**

Man 2:	**Excuse me, is there a gas [petrol] station near here?**
Woman 2:	**Umm, let me see. Do you see that big white building over there?**
Man 2:	**Yes.**
Woman 2:	**Well, that's a supermarket, and there's a gas [petrol] station right across from [opposite] it, on the corner.**
Man 2:	**Thank you.**
Woman 2:	**That's OK.**

Man 1:	**Excuse me.**
Woman 1:	**Sure. Can I help you?**
Man 1:	**Yes, please. Is there a drugstore [chemist] near here?**
Woman 1:	**Uh, yes. There's one on the next block next to the theater [theatre]. Do you see the Palace Theater [Theatre]?**
Man 1:	**Yes, I see it.**
Woman 1:	**Well, there's a drugstore [chemist] right next to it.**
Man 1:	**Thanks.**
Woman 1:	**You're welcome.**

3. WRITING ACTIVITY

Look at the map again and complete the conversation. Then listen to conversation 3 of Activity 2 again to check your answers.

Man: **Excuse me.**

Woman: **Sure, can I help you?**

Man: **Yes, please.** | Is | | a

drugstore [chemist] near here?

Woman: **Uh, yes,** | one on the | |

block, | | **the theater**

[theatre]. Do you see the Palace Theater [Theatre]?

Man: **Yes, I see it.**

Woman: **Well,** | a drugstore [chemist] right

| | it.

Man: **Thanks.**

Woman: **You're welcome.**

4. SPEAKING ACTIVITY

Based on the map from Activity 2, create sentences using the expressions below.

Example: The bank is to the left of the restaurant.

1. **across from [opposite]**

2. **next to**

3. **on the left**

4. **near**

5. **on the right**

6. **in front of**

7. **on the corner**

Ordinal Numbers

GRAMMAR

Ordinal numbers give the position or order of an object within a series.

first	1st	fourth	4th	seventh	7th	tenth	10th
second	2nd	fifth	5th	eighth	8th		
third	3rd	sixth	6th	ninth	9th		

5. SPEAKING ACTIVITY

Look at these two pictures. One shows how the area used to be thirty years ago. The other shows how it is now. How things are different now.

Example: (computer store, theater [theatre]) There's a computer store next to the theater [theatre] now.

1. **(bus stop, department store)**

2. **(supermarket, department store)**

3. **(some apartments, school)**

4. **(parking lot [car park], hotel)**

6. WRITING ACTIVITY

Look at the picture from the previous activity. Describe the buildings you see in the current picture from left to right. Use ordinal numbers.

Example:

The first building is...

GRAMMAR

There Is/There Are

Use *there is* with a singular noun. Use *there are* with a plural noun.
Both have the same meaning.

> There's a bank on that corner.

> There are some good hotels in Oxford.

For questions, use *Is there...?* and *Are there...?*

> Excuse me, is there a phone in the hotel?

> Are there any good restaurants near here?

Prepositions of Place

To say where a place is, use *in* and *on*.

> Her university's in London.

> There's a bank on the next block.

> It's not on the left; it's on the right.

> The children's clothes are on the third floor.

> My apartment is on 45th Street.

> There's a mailbox [post box] on the corner.

The Use of One and Some

Use *one* or *some* to avoid repeating a word.

> Is there a bus stop near here? Yes, there's one (= bus stop) over there.

> There's a gas [petrol] station here, and there's one (= gas [petrol] station) on the next block, too.

> There aren't any phones in the station, but there are some (= phones) in the hotel.

DID YOU KNOW?

Thirteen is considered an unlucky number in English-speaking cultures. The floors in many tall buildings, such as hotels, skip floor number thirteen. They go from twelve directly to fourteen.

7. WRITING ACTIVITY

Draw a map of your block or area. Are there restaurants? Banks? Is there a school? A bus stop?

After you draw your map, use *there is/there are* to describe each of the locations in your area.

A map of my area

Example:

The first building on my block is an apartment building. Next to the apartment building, there is a bank and then a restaurant. Then there are two more apartment buildings. Across the street, there is a small hotel, a gas station and a bus stop...

Check It!

Test what you learned in this lesson. Review anything you're not sure of.

CAN YOU . . . ?

☐ **get someone's attention**
Excuse me.

☐ **ask someone where something is located**
Is there a post office near here?
Is there a bank in the area?

☐ **say where things are in relation to each other**
The restaurant is next to the travel agency.
The Grand Hotel is just around the corner, and there's a post office next to it.

☐ **use ordinal numbers**
The second building is a computer store.
The third building is a department store.

☐ **use *there is/there are***
There's a bank on that corner.
There are some good hotels in Oxford.

☐ **use *in* and *on* to describe a place**
Her university's in London.
There's a bank on the next block.

☐ **use *one* and *some***
Is there a bus stop near here?
Yes, there's one over there.
There's a gas [petrol] station here, and there's one on the next block, too.

 BERLITZ HOTSPOT Go to www.berlitzhotspot.com for...

 Social Networking
Go to **Berlitz Hotspot** and tell us about your town. Is it small or large? Is everything close by or far away? How do you get around your town?

 Podcast 10
Excuse Me!
Download this podcast

Internet Activity
Are you interested in more practice describing locations? Go to **Berlitz Hotspot** to access a map of Los Angeles. Describe how the sites are located in relation to each other.

 Video 6 – Asking for Directions
A woman is lost. How does she approach someone and ask for directions? Where is the post office? Watch the video and learn how to ask for directions.

Lesson 11

Take the Second Left.

DIALOGUE

 Listen to these people asking for directions.

1.

Man 1:   **Excuse me, how do I get to the ABC Theater [Theatre]?**

Woman 1:   **The ABC? OK, do you see those traffic lights? Turn left there, and then take the second right. The theater's [theatre's] about two blocks down, on your right.**

Man 1:   **Thanks.**

Woman 1:   **You're welcome.**

2.

Woman 2:   **Excuse me, how do I get to Paddington Station from here? I'm lost!**

Man 2:   **It's OK, you're almost there! Take the first right, there...let me see...no, go straight ahead and take the fourth turning on your right. Then take the first left and carry straight on. You'll see the station on your left.**

Woman 2:   **Thanks a lot.**

1. DIALOGUE ACTIVITY

Where does each person want to go?

ABC Theater [Theatre]

Are the places they want to go to nearby or far away?

120

Use the following words and expressions to
guide you through the lesson.

VOCABULARY

about	road
about two blocks down	station
bridge	to stop
bus station	straight ahead
Can you tell me how to get to...?	street
down (to go down)	to take
to get (to)	to tell
to go	then
hill	through (to go through)
How do I get to...?	traffic light
lost	to turn
movie theater [cinema]	under
over (to go over)	up (to go up)
past (to go past)	

GRAMMAR

Spellings

In some cases, American and British English use different spellings.
For example, the American English word *color* is spelled [spelt] *colour* in
British English (similar examples are *theater/theatre*, *favorite/favourite*,
neighbor/neighbour). Some of these differences are irregular and can
only be learned—for example, the noun *practice* is the same in both
American and British English, but the verb is *practice* in American English
and *practise* in British English.

Different tenses of certain words are also spelled [spelt] differently.
For example, the past tense of *travel* is *traveled* in American English
but *travelled* in British English.

Words like *recognize* have z endings in American English but in British
English both z and s can be used (recognize/recognise).

121

2. LISTENING ACTIVITY

Listen to three people give directions to different places. Identify them on the map. Number the places 1, 2 and 3.

1.

Man 1:   **The bus station? Sure. See the black building on the right? Turn right just there, and then take the...one, two, three...take the third left. There's a hotel on the corner. Go straight ahead, and the bus station is on the left. It's across from [opposite] a small park.**

2.

Woman: **Sure, there's a post office near here. Do you see the movie theater [cinema] over there? Go straight ahead, past the supermarket. There's a post office next to the Grand Hotel.**

3.

Man 2:   **Yes, I know Forest Road. My friend lives there. Well, go straight ahead for three blocks, then turn left at the lights. Go straight ahead, and take the second right. There's a school on the corner on the left. But turn right there. Then take the first right, and that's Forest Road. Is that OK?**

3. WRITING ACTIVITY

What words are missing from the dialogue? Use the map to help you. Then listen to the directions in part 3 of Activity 2 to check your answers.

Yes, I know Forest Road. My friend lives there. Well, go | straight |

| ahead | **for three** | | **, then**

| | | | **at the lights. Go straight**

ahead, and take the | | | | **. There's**

a school on | | | | **on the left.**

But | | **right there. Then take** | |

| | | | **, and that's Forest Road. Is**

that OK?

4. SPEAKING ACTIVITY 66 99

Give directions to these places. Start at the point marked on the map for Activity 2.

1. **supermarket** | Go straight ahead |
   | for three blocks... |

3. **gas [petrol] station** | |
   | |

2. **post office** | |
   | |

4. **bus station** | |
   | |

5. LISTENING ACTIVITY

Some visitors are trying to find their way around by car. Listen to the conversation. Complete the sentences and put them in the correct order.

	Go	up	the hill.
	Go		post office.
1	Go		the bridge.

| | Go | | a park. |
| | Go | | a school. |

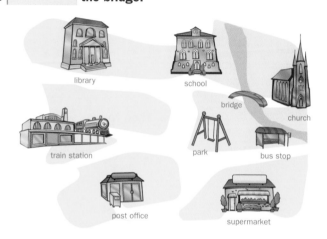

library

school

bridge

church

train station

park

bus stop

post office

supermarket

Wife:	Now let me see. Where are we? Ah yes. Turn left there.
Husband:	Here?
Wife:	No, don't turn left here! There, at the lights. Turn left at the lights.
Husband:	Sorry, dear.
Wife:	Now go straight ahead for a few blocks. Where's the bridge? Is there a bridge? Ah yes, there it is. Go over the bridge and past a school. Where's the school?
Son:	There! There's the school. On the right.
Wife:	Thank you, David. I see the school. Please be quiet.
Son:	Sorry!
Husband:	What do I do next? Do I go straight ahead up the hill?
Wife:	Just a moment. Yes, that's right. Up the hill. Then take the second right. No, don't turn right here! The second right!
Husband:	The second right at the lights?
Wife:	Yes, and then we go through the park, turn right, go past the post office, and then there's the...oh where's the hotel? Where are we?
Son:	We're lost!

     GRAMMAR

When giving instructions, we do not need to say *you* before the verb.

> Go straight ahead for two blocks.
>
> Do you see that hotel? Turn left there.
>
> Take the second street on the right.

When we tell someone not to do something, we put *don't* before the verb.

> Don't go through the park.
>
> The traffic light is green—don't stop!

6. WRITING ACTIVITY

Make the following directions negative.

1. **Walk to the traffic lights and turn right.**

   > **Don't walk to the traffic lights and turn right.**

2. **Go through the park and turn left.**

3. **Go straight ahead for two blocks.**

4. **Go past the post office.**

5. **Turn right then go straight for three blocks.**

7. ACTIVITY

Draw a map of a small town. Use all the vocabulary that you know so far. Include the following: a school, a gas [petrol] station, a department store, a restaurant, an apartment building, houses, a park, a bank, a coffee shop, bus stops, a bridge, traffic lights, etc. Label everything on the map in English.

Small
town
map

8. SPEAKING ACTIVITY "

Give directions from place to place on the map. Also give some directions in the negative. Prepare your answers by writing down some of the directions.

To get to the restaurant from the bridge, don't turn left at the bank.

It's faster to cross through the park.

Punctuation   **GRAMMAR**

Some punctuation differs between American and British English. Here are a few examples:

Double quotation marks ("word") are used in American English but single quotation marks are used in British English ('word').

If a word appears in quotation marks at the end of a clause or sentence, the comma or full point appears within the quotation mark in American English ("word,"/"word.") but outside the quotation mark in British English ('word',/'word'.)

Clauses separated by a dash have a long dash (—) with no spaces in American English and a shorter, spaced dash in British English (–).

Check It!

Test what you learned in this lesson and review anything you're not sure of.

CAN YOU . . . ?

☐ **ask for directions**
Excuse me, how do I get to the ABC Theater [Theatre]?
Excuse me, how do I get to Paddington Station from here?

☐ **understand directions**
The ABC? OK, do you see those traffic lights? Turn left there, and then take the second right. The theater's [theatre's] about two blocks down on your right.
Go straight ahead and take the fourth turning on your right. Then take the first left and carry straight on. You'll see the station on your left.

☐ **give instructions**
Go straight ahead for two blocks.
Do you see that hotel? Turn left there.

☐ **tell someone not to do something**
Don't go through the park.
The traffic light is green—don't stop!

BERLITZ HOTSPOT   Go to www.berlitzhotspot.com for...

Social Networking
Share your local culture with your Hotspot friends. What's the most important site to visit in your town? How do you get there from where you live?

Podcast 11
Understanding Directi‹
Download this podcast

Internet Activity
Are you interested in learning more about large North American or British cities? Use your favorite [favourite] search engine to access a city you'd like to visit. Select a handful of tourist attractions that seem interesting to you, and look at a city map. Explain how to get from one site to another.

Lesson 12

What Time Do You Close?

LESSON OBJECTIVES

Lesson 12 is about time. When you finish this lesson, you'll know how to:

- ask about opening and closing hours
- talk about schedules

DIALOGUE

 Listen to these people ask about when different places are open.

Taylor Sports Shop. Can I help you?

Yes, please. Are you open tomorrow?

No, I'm sorry, Madam. It's Sunday tomorrow, so we're closed. We're closed on Sunday and Monday.

And Monday? Oh, I see. Thank you.

Excuse me, what days are you closed?

The pool is open every day, but on Wednesdays and Thursdays it's closed in the evenings.

Thanks.

Are the post offices open on the weekends?

No, they're closed on Saturday afternoons and Sundays.

Oh, dear.

130

Use the following words and expressions to guide you through the lesson.

VOCABULARY

to close	place
closed	pool
day	quarter
every	question
flea market	tomorrow
hour(s)	tour
midnight	until
money	week
open	weekend
to open	zoo

DAYS OF THE WEEK

Monday	Friday
Tuesday	Saturday
Wednesday	Sunday
Thursday	

1. DIALOGUE ACTIVITY

What are the places the people are asking about?

a sports shop

When are the places closed?

2. **LISTENING ACTIVITY**

 Listen to three people ask about what time different places are open. Label them 1, 2 and 3 in the order you hear them.

Then look at the signs again. Say what time the stores open and close. Follow the example.

Example: Dickens Department Store is open from 10:00 a.m. (ten) to 6:15 p.m. (six-fifteen).

1.

Man:	**Excuse me. What are your hours, please?**
Woman:	**We're open from six-thirty to eleven forty-five.**
Man:	**Eleven forty-five. Thank you.**
Woman:	**You're welcome.**

2.

Man:	**Can I help you?**
Woman:	**Yes. What time do you close today, please?**
Man:	**At six-fifteen. We're open until six-fifteen.**
Woman:	**Thanks.**

3.

Man:	**Hello, hello.**
Woman:	**I'm sorry. We're closed.**
Man:	**Yes, I know. But what time do you open this evening, please?**
Woman:	**We open at eight-twenty. Eight-twenty until two a.m.**
Man:	**Right. Thanks.**

3. LISTENING ACTIVITY

Listen to this woman ask about when certain sights are open. Fill in the times and days the places are open on the chart.

Location	Days Open	Opening Times	
Flea Market		from	to
Empire State Building		from	to
Bronx Zoo Tour		from	to
Beautiful Bronx Bus Tour		from	to

Man: **Good afternoon, madam. Can I help you?**

Woman: **Yes, please. I have some questions about the hours of these places.**

Man: **OK. Go ahead.**

Woman: **Uh, first the flea market...**

Man: **The flea market is only open on Sundays.**

Woman: **Oh, I see. From what time?**

Man: **From ten a.m. to five-thirty.**

Woman: **Five-thirty. OK. And the Empire State Building? Is it open every day?**

Man: **Yes, it is. It's open from nine-thirty until twelve o'clock midnight every day.**

Woman: **Now, the tour. The Bronx Zoo tour—what day is that?**

Man: **The zoo tour is only on Saturdays, from nine a.m. to four p.m.**

Woman: **Only on Saturday? That's no good. What's this? The beautiful Bronx bus tour. What day is that?**

Man: **The beautiful Bronx tour is on Tuesdays, Wednesdays and Thursdays from 8 a.m. to 1 o'clock.**

Woman: **Eight to one Tuesdays, Wednesdays and Thursdays. That's good! How much is it?**

Man: **It's twenty-five dollars per person.**

Woman: **OK. Thanks.**

4. WRITING ACTIVITY

Look at the chart for Activity 3. Write the questions that correspond to the answers.

1. | **Is the Empire State Building open every day?** |

   Yes, it is. It's open every day.

2. | |

   No, it's only open on Sundays.

3. | |

   At 10:00 a.m.

4. | |

   Only on Saturdays.

5. | |

   $25.00.

Prepositions of Time

We use *at* when we talk about something that happens at a specific time.

> The store opens at 9:15.
>
> I'm sorry, but this restaurant closes at midnight.

From and *to* indicate a period of time.

> The market is open from 8:00 a.m. to 6:00 p.m.
>
> We're open from Monday to Friday.

We use *on* with the days of the week.

> We're open on Saturdays, but we're closed on Sundays.

Note that in this example the day of the week is plural. This is because we are talking about something that happens regularly.

5. READING ACTIVITY

Read the short text about Karen's daily schedule. Then explain your daily schedule.

My name is Karen and I teach Spanish at a high school.
I have the same schedule every day during the week:
I start at 8:00 a.m. and finish at 4:00 p.m. Though in winter,
I help with the girls' basketball team. We have practice on
Wednesday nights from 5:00 to 6:30 p.m.

I am very active, so I try to go to the gym. I usually go on
Mondays, Tuesdays and Thursdays from 6:30 a.m. to 7:30 a.m.
If I can't go in the morning, I go for an hour after school.
I like to have my weekends free. I try not to make plans so
that I can relax and enjoy my free time. On Saturdays,
I always sleep late.

6. WRITING ACTIVITY

Read Jamie's blog and fill in the missing prepositions where necessary.

Jamie's blog

About Me | Contact | Fun Ideas | Recent News

Man, I hate Mondays. I am a late sleeper, so when my alarm rings **at** 7:00 a.m. _____ Monday mornings, it drives me crazy. I feel like sleeping _____ another four hours! But, I have to get up _____ 7:00 a.m., so I can take a shower, drink a quick coffee and be _____ the corner _____ the bus stop to catch my bus _____ 7:30 a.m. Though I don't live too far away _____ my job, it takes _____ 30 minutes to get there. I start _____ 8:00 a.m. Monday to Friday on the dot. I work as a secretary. I work _____ 8:00 a.m. _____ 5:00 p.m., and I have one hour to eat my lunch. I usually go _____ 12:00 p.m. _____ 1:00 p.m. sometimes I have to go _____ 12 because I am just too hungry! The only good thing about starting early _____ the morning is that I finish early _____ the afternoon. In the afternoons, I usually like to take my dog to the park. We are usually there every day _____ 6:00 _____ 7:00 p.m. Sometimes afterwards, I meet up with some friends, or go to the library or maybe watch some T.V. On [At] weekends, I like to spend time with friends, go shopping or go to the beach. I wish every day were Saturday _____ Sunday!

© Jamie's Blog 2010   Home | About Me | Contact | Fun Ideas | Recent News

Rhythm and Stress

PRONUNCIATION

When we speak, we stress some words more than others. The words we stress are important to our meaning. Usually, these words are nouns, verbs, adjectives, or adverbs. These are sometimes called content words. The stress falls on the most important syllable of these words. Generally, this syllable is the one that receives normal word stress.

7. LISTENING ACTIVITY

 Listen to these sentences. Can you hear the difference between the stressed syllables and the unstressed syllables? The stressed syllables are written in capital letters.

1. Turn LEFT at the CORner.

2. Go OVER the BRIDGE.

3. Take the FIRST street on the RIGHT.

4. We OPEN at NINE o'clock.

5. There's a BANK on the LEFT.

8. LISTENING ACTIVITY

 Listen to the following sentences. Circle the stressed words or syllables.

1. We're closed on(Sundays)and(Mondays).

2. It's not on the left it's on the right.

3. Don't go through the park.

4. The watches are on the fourth floor.

5. Excuse me, what time do you close?

LEARNING TIP

 As you drive or bike around, or take the dog for a walk, think about the directions you are following. Tell yourself in English where to go (turn right, take the second right, stop at the corner).

Check It!

Test what you learned in this lesson and review anything you're not sure of.

CAN YOU . . . ?

☐ **ask for opening/closing times**
Are you open tomorrow?
Excuse me, what days are you closed?

☐ **give opening/closing times/days**
The pool is open every day, but on Wednesdays and Thursdays it's closed in the evenings.
No, the post offices are closed on Saturday afternoons and Sundays.

☐ **name the days of the week**
Sunday   Thursday
Monday   Friday
Tuesday   Saturday
Wednesday

☐ **use prepositions of time**
The store opens at 9:15.
The market is open from 8:00 a.m. to 6:00 p.m.
We're open on Saturdays, but we're closed on Sundays.

☐ **identify the stressed syllables in a sentence**
Turn LEFT at the CORner.
Go over the BRIDGE.

Learn More ✚

Collect and read English-language brochures for hotels and tourist attractions. They often give written instructions, as well as maps, showing how to get there. See how many of the instructions you recognize. Look at the map and see if you can find the words for river, street, avenue, etc.

BERLITZ HOTSPOT   Go to www.berlitzhotspot.com for...

 Social Networking
You told us what the most important site was to visit in your town on **Berlitz Hotspot**. Now tell us about that site's opening/closing times and days, so that your Hotspot friends can visit some day!

Podcast 12
We're Open 24/7
Download this podcast.

 Internet Activity
Time to practice [practise] talking about schedules. Go back to the tourist attractions that you selected for the Internet Activity in Lesson 11. Find out what time they open and close. Practice [Practise] giving the sites' schedules aloud.

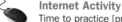

Lesson 13

I'm Just Looking.

Lesson 13 is about shopping. When you finish this lesson, you'll know how to:

- accept or refuse help in a store
- understand shopping announcements

DIALOGUE

 Listen to these people shop for electronics.

Customer 1:	**Excuse me, do you carry [stock] computers?**
Salesclerk 1:	**Yes, we do. They're on the second floor.**
Salesclerk 2:	**Are you being helped [served]?**
Customer 2:	**Oh. I'm looking for camcorders.**
Salesclerk 2:	**Sorry. We don't carry [stock] any video cameras.**
Customer 3:	**Excuse me. We're looking for a DVD player.**
Salesclerk 3:	**Just a second, ma'am. I'm helping this lady.**
Customer 3:	**Oh, sorry.**

1. DIALOGUE ACTIVITY

What were some of the items the customers ask for?

computers

Does the store carry [stock] the items?

Use the following words and expressions to
guide you through the lesson.

VOCABULARY

all	jacket
answering machine	to look for
anymore [any more]	May/Can I help you (with something)?
attention	MP3 player
to be on sale	to need
to buy	to pay for
camcorder	percent [per cent]
to carry [to stock]	to pick out
CD player	purchases
clothing	sale
computer	shirt
department	shoe
door	(pair of) shoes
Do you have/sell/carry [stock]…?	to shop
DVD player	shopper
foot/feet	Someone is (already) helping me.
to go on	special
half-price	tired
help, to	today
I'm (already) being helped [served].	toy
I'm just looking.	to try on
I'm looking for…	video camera
Is someone helping you?	to wear
item	

DID YOU KNOW?

American stores
regularly have sales.
British stores also have
sales throughout the
year, but especially in
January and July.

DID YOU KNOW?

Salespeople in the U.S. and U.K.
are generally very helpful. You can
ask them about the location, size,
price, quality, etc., of an item.
If you can't find a salesperson,
visit the Customer Service center
[centre] of the store.

141

2. LISTENING ACTIVITY

 Listen to these announcements in a large department store. Write the number of each announcement next to the announcement below.

1. **Attention shoppers! It's 6 p.m. We're closing for the day. Please complete all your purchases. Thank you for shopping at Field's.**

2. **Attention shoppers! Today we're having a special sale on all toys. Twenty-five to fifty percent [per cent] off all items! That's right. Everything in our toy department is on sale, today only!**

3. **Attention shoppers! Our clothing sale is going on right now [taking place now] on the fifth floor. That's right. Everything is on sale in our clothing department on the fifth floor.**

4. **Attention shoppers! We're looking for a lost boy. His name is Bobby. He's four years old. He's wearing a blue jacket.**

5. **Attention shoppers! Are your feet tired? Maybe you need a new pair of shoes. We're having a half-price sale on all shoes, today only. Come and try on a pair or two!**

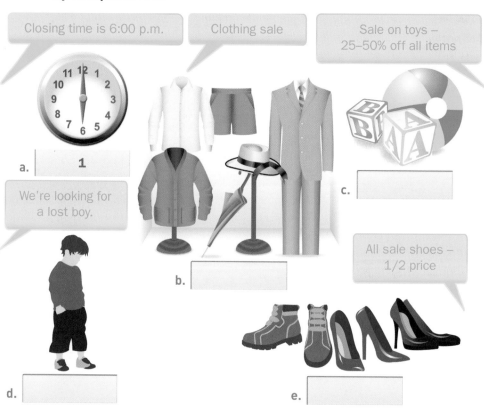

Closing time is 6:00 p.m.

Clothing sale

Sale on toys – 25–50% off all items

a. 1

We're looking for a lost boy.

c.

b.

All sale shoes – 1/2 price

d.

e.

142

3. LISTENING ACTIVITY

Listen to the announcements again and fill in the missing information.

1.   Announcer: **Attention shoppers! It's** [6] **p.m. We're**

[   ] **for the day. Please complete all your**

[   ] **. Thank you for shopping at Field's.**

2.   Announcer: **Attention** [   ] **! Today we're having a special**

[   ] **on all toys. Twenty-five to fifty percent**

[per cent] [   ] **all items! That's right. Everything**

in our toy department is [   ] [   ] **,**

today only!

3.   Announcer: **Attention shoppers! Our clothing sale is going on right now**

[taking place now] on the [   ] **floor. That's right.**

Everything is on sale in our clothing [   ] **on the**

fifth floor.

4.   Announcer: **Attention shoppers! We're looking for a lost** [   ] **.**

His name is Bobby. He's four years old. He's wearing a

[   ] [   ] **.**

5.   Announcer: **Attention shoppers! Are your feet tired? Maybe you need a new**

[   ] **of shoes. We're having a** [   ]

[   ] **sale on all shoes, today only. Come and try on**

a pair or two!

The Present Continuous Tense   GRAMMAR

Form the present continuous tense using: *to be* (am, is, are) + *verb -ing*

    I am working.

    He is going.

We use the present continuous tense to talk about something that is happening exactly at the moment of speaking:

    It's 6:30. We're closing now.

    Are you looking for the children's department?

We also use it when something takes place in the present, but not necessarily at the exact moment of speaking:

    Ava has a new job. She's working at a supermarket.

We often use the present continuous tense to talk about a period of time in the present: today, this morning, etc.

    They're having a sale at the department store this week.

4. WRITING ACTIVITY

Write five statements in the present continuous that are true right now.

Example: Right now, I'm studying English.

1. _____

2. _____

3. _____

4. _____

5. _____

5. SPEAKING ACTIVITY

Make up five announcements using the words in parentheses using the present continuous.

Example: (all, MP3 players) Attention shoppers! We are having a special sale today. All MP3 players are 50% off. Yes, 50% off! Take advantage of this special offer.

1. **(be on sale, CD player)**

2. **(clothing department, half-price)**

3. **(feet, shoes, today)**

4. **(toy, special, percent [per cent])**

5. **(jacket, need, try on)**

6. WRITING ACTIVITY

What are they doing? Write down what each person is doing.

1. **They are buying a TV.**

2.

3.

4.

7. WRITING ACTIVITY

Two friends run into each other at a clothing store in the men's department. Complete the dialogue. Fill in the correct form of the verbs below. The same verb may be used more than once.

to be	to do	to buy	to shop	to work

Jennifer: **Teresa! Hi! What** [are] **you** [____] **here?**

Teresa: **Hi, Jennifer. I'm** [____] **a shirt for my boyfriend.**

Jennifer: **Oh,** [____] **you usually** [____] **for him?**

Teresa: **Not usually, but he** [____] [____] **late**

everyday [every day] this week, so I'm [____] **him a**

favor [favour].

146

8. WRITING ACTIVITY

Write sentences in the present continuous. Use the verbs below.

1. **(to buy)** — **I am buying a computer today.**

2. **(to help)** —

3. **(to look for)** —

4. **(to pay for)** —

5. **(to shop)** —

9. WRITING ACTIVITY

Imagine an interaction in a store between a salesclerk [sales assistant] and two different customers. Use the prompts or create your own conversation.

Salesclerk: **Can I help you?**

Ask if you can help the customer.

Customer 1:

Ask if they carry [stock] a particular item.

Salesclerk:

Say whether the store does/does not carry [stock] the item.

Customer 1:

If the store carries [stocks] the item, ask to see the selection. If the store does not carry [stock] the item, thank the salesclerk [sales assistant].

Customer 2:

Ask a salesclerk [sales assistant] for help.

Salesclerk:

Say that you can help the customer.

Customer 2:

Tell the salesclerk [sales assistant] what you are looking for.

Salesclerk:

Respond accordingly.

Check It!

Test what you learned in this lesson and review anything you're not sure of.

CAN YOU . . . ?

☐ **ask for help in a store**
Excuse me, do you carry [stock] computers?
Excuse me. We're looking for DVD players.

☐ **refuse help in a store**
No thanks, we're just looking.

☐ **talk about special prices in a store**
There's a sale on DVDs.
They're half price.
They're 20% off.

☐ **use the present continuous tense**
I am working.
He is going.

☐ **use the present continuous tense to talk about something that is happening exactly at the moment of speaking**
He's busy now. He's helping another customer.
They're having a sale at Macy's department store this week.

 BERLITZ HOTSPOT   Go to www.berlitzhotspot.com for...

 Social Networking
Have you ever gone shopping in the United States or the United Kingdom? Go to **Berlitz Hotspot** and share your stories with your Hotspot friends.

 Podcast 13
Types of Stores
Download this podcast

 Internet Activity
Are you interested in practicing [practising] what you've learned? Go to **Berlitz Hotspot** for a list of links to American and British stores. Take a look and make up small dialogues. Practice [Practise] naming items, talk about prices and special sales.

Lesson 14

I'd Like Something...

149

DIALOGUE

 Listen to these customers in a clothing store.

1.

Customer 1:   **Excuse me. Can I try this blouse on?**

Salesclerk 1:   **Certainly. The dressing room is right over there.**

Customer 1:   **Thanks...Oh, this one is too small. It's really tight on me. Well, do you have a bigger one? Maybe a size 12.**

Salesclerk 1:   **Let's see. Oh, you're in luck. There's one left.**

2.

Salesclerk 2:   **This jacket looks great on you.**

Customer 2:   **Really? Well, it's a little expensive though. Do you have anything less expensive?**

Salesclerk 2:   **Yes, we do. But this one is made for you.**

Customer 2:   **Well, let me think about it.**

3.

Salesclerk 3:   **Would you like to try that skirt on?**

Customer 3:   **Um, I don't think so. It's a little too short. I'd like something longer.**

Salesclerk 3:   **Well, this one is longer. And I think it's a better color [colour] for you.**

Customer 3:   **Yes. I think you're right. I'll take it.**

DID YOU KNOW?

Women's clothing sizes in the U.S. and U.K. are slightly different—for example, a size 12 in the U.S. is one size larger than a size 12 in the U.K. And shoe sizes are very different!

Use the following words and expressions to
guide you through the lesson.

aisle	less
attractive	light
to be in luck	long
to be left	to look good/bad on
to be made for (you)	loud
because	luck
behind	mirror
belt	more
better	narrow
blouse	pants [trousers]
bright	short
certainly	skirt
coat	stylish
dark	tie
dressing room	tight
to fit	too
great	vest
hat	to want
heavy	wide

1. DIALOGUE ACTIVITY

What items are the customers considering?

> a blouse

>

>

Which customer actually buys the item?

>

2. LISTENING ACTIVITY

Listen to the conversations from Activity 1 again. Fill in the missing information.

1.

Customer: **Excuse me. Can I** [try] **this blouse on?**

Salesclerk: **Certainly. The** [＿＿＿＿] [＿＿＿＿] **is right over there.**

Customer: **Thanks...Oh, this one is too** [＿＿＿＿]**. It's really** [＿＿＿＿] **on me. Well, do you have a** [＿＿＿＿] **one? Maybe a size 12?**

Salesclerk: **Let's see.**

2.

Salesclerk: **This jacket looks** [＿＿＿＿] **on you.**

Customer: **Really? Well, it's a little** [＿＿＿＿] **though. Do you have anything** [＿＿＿＿] [＿＿＿＿]**?**

Salesclerk: **Yes, we do. But this one is made for you.**

Customer: **Well, let me think about it.**

3.

Salesclerk: **Would you like to try that skirt on?**

Customer: **Um, I don't think so. It's a little too** [＿＿＿＿]**. I'd like something** [＿＿＿＿]**.**

Salesclerk: **Well, this one is** [＿＿＿＿]**. And I think it's a** [＿＿＿＿] **color [colour] for you.**

Customer: **Yes. I think you're right. I'll take it.**

Comparative Forms of Adjectives

GRAMMAR

Add *–er* or *–r* to compare one- and some two-syllable adjectives.

cheap	cheaper
large	larger

Most adjectives with three syllables use *more* (+) or *less* (–).

more attractive	less expensive

If a two-syllable adjective ends in *–y*, the *–y* changes to *–ier*.

heavy	heavier

If it ends in *–ple* or *–ble*, add *–r*.

simple	simpler

Other spelling changes:

big	bigger
fat	fatter

Irregular forms:

good	better
bad	worse

Remember that in English, the adjective comes before the noun:
a bigger shirt.

DID YOU KNOW?

In English, some words can have more than one meaning. For example, "loud" often means "noisy" but "loud" also means very bright in color [colour] (see Activity 5 for an example). When you come across a word you know that doesn't make sense in the sentence, use context clues—the other words in the sentence or paragraph—to help you figure out the meaning of the word. You can also refer to an online or learner's dictionary.

3. WRITING ACTIVITY

Change the following adjectives to their comparative form.

1. **attractive**   more attractive

2. **bright**

3. **dark**

4. **fat**

5. **great**

6. **heavy**

7. **light**

8. **long**

9. **loud**

10. **narrow**

11. **short**

12. **stylish**

13. **tight**

14. **wide**

15. **big**

4. LISTENING ACTIVITY

Listen to some customers shop for clothes. What does each one want?

Customer 1 wants   a smaller shirt .

Customer 2 wants .

Customer 3 wants .

Customer 1: **This shirt doesn't fit me well. It's too big.**

Salesclerk 1: **Oh? Try this one then. It's smaller.**

Customer 1: **OK. Thanks.**

Customer 2: **These pants [trousers] are very expensive.**

Salesclerk 2: **Well, we have some cheaper ones down the next aisle.**

Customer 3: **This is a nice skirt, but it's a little long.**

Salesclerk 3: **Do you want to try on a shorter one?**

Customer 3: **Yes.**

5. LISTENING ACTIVITY

 Listen to some more people shopping for clothes. Why aren't they buying the items? Match each situation with its corresponding reason.

1. **He's not buying the belt because**   a. **it's too loud.**

2. **She's not buying the coat because**   b. **she wants a brighter one.**

3. **She's not buying the hat because**   c. **it's too heavy.**

4. **He's not buying the tie because**   d. **he wants a wider one.**

Salesclerk 1: **Do you want this belt, sir?**

Customer 1: **No, I don't think so. It's too narrow. I want something a little wider.**

Salesclerk 2: **Are you taking the coat, ma'am? It looks good on you.**

Customer 2: **Oh, really? No, I don't think so. It's too heavy. I need something lighter.**

Salesclerk 3: **Do you like this hat, ma'am?**

Customer 3: **Well, not really. I don't like the color [colour]. It's too dark. I'd like something brighter.**

Salesclerk 4: **This is a nice tie, sir.**

Customer 4: **Oh, no, no, no. That's too loud for me.**

6. WRITING ACTIVITY

Look at the pairs of pictures. For each pair, write a sentence using a comparative form.

1. **The color [colour] of the first shirt is brighter.**

4.

2.

5.

3.

7. SPEAKING ACTIVITY "

Now you are shopping in a clothing store. Read the prompts and write down what you are going to say. Then join in the dialogue.

Salesclerk: **Can I help you?**

You:
> **Yes. Do you carry [stock] jeans?**

Say yes. Ask if they carry [stock] jeans.

Salesclerk: **Jeans? Uh, oh yes, we do. Right over here. These are quite nice. They're $89 [£55].**

You:

Tell him it's too expensive. Ask if he has anything a little less expensive.

Salesclerk: **Let's see. Well, here's something for $55 [£34].**

You:

Ask if you can try them on.

Salesclerk: **Certainly. There's a mirror right behind you.**

You:

Tell him you like them, and you'll take them.

Salesclerk: **Very good.**

DID YOU KNOW?

Some nouns, though singular, are always written in plural form and take a plural verb.
jeans ⟶ Your jeans are nice.
pants [trousers] ⟶ The pants [trousers] were washed.
scissors ⟶ These scissors are sharp.

Check It!

Test what you learned in this lesson and review anything you're not sure of.

CAN YOU . . . ?

☐ **make statements about clothing**
Oh, this one is too small.
This skirt's really tight on me.
This jacket's a little expensive.

☐ **form comparatives**
cheap ⟶ cheaper
more attractive/less attractive
heavy ⟶ heavier

☐ **use irregular comparatives**
good ⟶ better
bad ⟶ worse

BERLITZ HOTSPOT   Go to www.berlitzhotspot.com for...

Social Networking
Tell your Hotspot friends what you are wearing today!

Podcast 14
Formal and Informal Clothing
Download this podcast

Internet Activity
Are you interested in more practice with clothing? Go to **Berlitz Hotspot** for links to some American and British clothing stores. Look through the catalogues, and identify the items you see by item type and description (color [colour], length, etc.). Say which items you want and what size and color [colour] you want them in.

Video 7 – The Clothing Shop
It's time to try on some clothes. How does the shopper ask the salesclerk [sales assistant] for help? Do the clothes fit well? Watch the video and learn how to find a dressing room and request clothes in another size.

Lesson 15

Do You Take Credit Cards?

LESSON OBJECTIVES

Lesson 15 is about making purchases at the shopping mall [centre]. When you finish this lesson, you'll know how to:

- talk about forms of payment
- use comparatives: *more than* and *less than*

DIALOGUE

Listen to these people making purchases.

1.

Salesclerk 1:   **How would you like to pay?**

Customer 1:   **Do you accept credit cards?**

Salesclerk 1:   **Yes, sir, we do.**

Customer 1:   **Here you go.**

Salesclerk 1:   **Thanks. Just a second. Could you please sign here, sir?**

Customer 1:   **Sure.**

2.

Salesclerk 2:   **Cash or charge, ma'am?**

Customer 2:   **Oh, uh, don't you take checks [cheques]?**

Salesclerk 2:   **No, I'm sorry.**

Customer 2:   **Oh, OK. Just a second. I think I have enough cash with me.**

3.

Salesclerk 3:   **How are you paying, sir?**

Customer 3:   **Uh, by check [cheque].**

Salesclerk 3:   **Fine. May I see some identification?**

Customer 3:   **Here's my employee ID card.**

Salesclerk 3:   **Oh. Well, would you mind showing me your driver's license [driving licence], if you have one?**

Customer 3:   **Oh, yeah. Here.**

Use the following words and expressions to
guide you through the lesson.

VOCABULARY

to accept	identification (ID)
cash	jewelry [jewellery]
charge	price
check [cheque]	ring
to cost	scarf (scarves, plural)
credit card	to show
debit card	silver
diamond	to sign
dress	suit
driver's license [driving licence]	sweater [cardigan or jumper]
employee	to take
enough	than
gold	

1. DIALOGUE ACTIVITY

How does each customer want to pay?

by credit card

DID YOU KNOW?

Both American and British English use decimals rather than commas when
writing prices or when communicating fractions of numbers. The symbol
for dollars is $ and for pounds sterling is £, followed by the amount (e.g.,
$2.50, £4.99).

DID YOU KNOW?

Checks [cheques] can be used to pay for goods in stores in the U.S.,
but in most other English-speaking countries they are being replaced by
electronic payment cards.

2. LISTENING ACTIVITY

Numbers 101–1,000. Listen to the prices of the items pictured. Then practice [practise] saying them yourself.

Comparing Items

When comparing two things, we use *than* after the comparative form of the adjective.

> The green coat is cheaper than the red one.
>
> The white shirt is more attractive than the blue shirt.

After *than* we usually use subject pronouns: *I, he, she, we, they,* etc.

> They are wealthier than we.
>
> He's older than I.
>
> I'm taller than she.

DID YOU KNOW?

You may hear, in informal speech, the object pronoun used after *than*. For example:
He's older than me.
I'm taller than her.
However, in formal written English, the subject pronoun should be used.

3. SPEAKING ACTIVITY

 Read the following prices aloud. Pay attention to your pronunciation. Check the recording to see how you're doing.

1. $272.⁰⁰

2. $431.⁹⁹

3. $512.⁰⁰

4. $620.⁰⁰

5. $703.⁸⁶

6. $844.⁰⁰

7. $924.⁹⁹

8. $989.⁰⁰

4. SPEAKING ACTIVITY 66 99

Compare the prices of the items in Activity 2. Use *more* or *less* and *than*.

Example:

scarf—red/yellow	The red scarf is less expensive than the yellow one.

1. **sweater [cardigan/ jumper]—green/white**

2. **dress—black/pink**

3. **ring—gold/diamond**

4. **suit—blue/black**

5. WRITING ACTIVITY

Use the following sentences to create a short dialogue.

1. **I'd like to pay by check [cheque].**

2. **I don't have a driver's license [driving licence].**

3. **Do you take credit cards?**

4. **I'll take the blue coat. It's more attractive than the red one.**

5. **Do you have anything less expensive than this one?**

Salesperson:	Here's a blue coat in size 12.
You:	Do you have anything less expensive than this one?
Salesperson:	
You:	
Salesperson:	
You:	

Salesperson:	
You:	
Salesperson:	
You:	

6. SPEAKING ACTIVITY ❝❞

What are your preferences? Answer the following questions with a comparative.

Example:

What are your favorite [favourite] colors [colours]?

I like bright colors [colours] better [more] than light colors [colours].

1. **Do you like the color [colour] blue or the color [colour] red better [more]?**

2. **Do you like to wear sandals or shoes?**

3. **Do you like to wear pants [trousers] or dresses?**

4. **Do you like to wear hats or ties?**

5. **Do you like to wear sweaters [cardigans/jumpers] or jackets?**

6. **Do you like gold or silver jewelry [jewellery]?**

7. SPEAKING ACTIVITY

Compare yourself to the people in the pictures. Use the formula *comparative + than + subject pronoun*.

Example: She is older than I am.

LEARNING TIP

Don't look at the answer key when you do the exercises. Try to answer even if you are not sure if you are correct.

Only refer to the answer key once you have made an attempt to say the answer aloud or write it down.

GRAMMAR

When Americans in particular speak quickly or informally, unemphasized words, or words that do not receive stress, become reduced. That is, the vowel sounds are not as long, and some consonants (such as initial *h*) reduce or even disappear. This is often the case with pronouns that begin with *h*.

I see'im! = I see him!

Do you trust'er? = Do you trust her?

8. LISTENING ACTIVITY

 Listen to the reductions in these examples:

1. **What is he buying?**

2. **Let her see the dress.**

3. **Does he mind paying by check [cheque]?**

Now which do you hear, "a" or "b"?

1. a. **Give him the money.**   b. **Give them the money.**

2. a. **Is he just looking?**   b. **Is she just looking?**

3. a. **Is her check [cheque] good?**   b. **Is our check [cheque] good?**

9. LISTENING ACTIVITY

 Listen to the following sentences with reduced pronouns. Then repeat each one quickly. Note that if you speak slowly, you should not reduce the pronouns.

I'm buying her a scarf.   **Give the jacket to him.**

Take her check [cheque].   **Can I try on his coat?**

Does he want to buy it?

Check It!

Test what you learned in this lesson. Review anything you're not sure of.

CAN YOU . . . ?

☐ **talk about forms of payment**
Do you accept credit cards?
I'm paying by check [cheque].
I'll pay in cash.

☐ **say the numbers to 1000**
$272
$703.86
$989

☐ **compare two or more things**
The green coat is cheaper than the red one.
The white shirt is more attractive than the blue shirt.

☐ **use subject pronouns after comparatives**
They are wealthier than we.
He's older than I.
I'm taller than she.

☐ **reduce unstressed words in fast speech**
What is he buying?
Let her see the dress.

Learn More +

Look at the ads that appear in English-language newspapers and magazines. See how many of the pictured items you can name in English. Make a list of items and any adjectives that can be used to describe them, for example, an unbreakable toy.

BERLITZ HOTSPOT Go to www.berlitzhotspot.com for...

 Social Networking
Go to **Berlitz Hotspot** and share your opinions on fashion with your Hotspot friends. Tell them which items you like more than others, such as *I like sandals better [more] than shoes.*

 Podcast 15
I'll Pay By...
Download this podcast

 Internet Activity
For more practice using the comparative, return to the link to the American and British clothing stores at **Berlitz Hotspot**. Look through the catalogues, and compare items using comparatives and *more/less...than.*

Lesson 16

Getting Around

DIALOGUE

 Listen to some people talk about how they travel to work.

 Where do you work?

 I work right here in Rockefeller Center.

 And where do you live?

 I live outside the city.

 How do you get to work?

 I take the train, and then I take the subway [underground].

 How long does it take?

 It takes about an hour and a half.

 How do you get to work?

 I take the bus.

 And what time do you leave?

 I leave at eight or eight-fifteen. It takes about 35 minutes, more or less.

 I go by car to work.

 And how long does it take?

 Oh, about an hour or so.

Use the following words and expressions to guide you through the lesson.

VOCABULARY

almost	**line** (subway [underground] line)
before	**more or less**
bike (bicycle)	**motorcycle**
bus	**on foot**
by (transportation [transport])	**outside**
change subway [underground] lines	**to ride**
to come	**right here**
convenient	**station**
to drive	**subway [underground]**
fast	**to take**
to get (to)	**taxi**
to go	**traffic**
half (half hour)	**train**
home	**trip**
How do you get to...?	**to wait**
How long does it take...?	**to walk**
It takes about...	**work**
to leave	

1. DIALOGUE ACTIVITY

How do each of the people get to work?

> The first man takes the train and the subway [underground].

>

>

How long does it take them?

>

>

>

2. LISTENING ACTIVITY

 Now listen to five more people talk about how they get to work, school or college. Match the two sentences each person says. Then check your answers by reading the text below.

1. **I ride my motorcycle to work.**   a. **It takes about five minutes.**

2. **I walk to school.**   b. **It's very convenient.**

3. **I drive to work.**   c. **It takes about ten minutes.**

4. **I go by bike.**   d. **It's very fast.**

5. **I take a taxi.**   e. **It takes about an hour and a half.**

Man 1: **I ride my motorcycle to work. It's very fast.**

Boy: **I don't take the bus to school. I walk to school. It takes about five minutes.**

Woman: **I drive to work. It's a long trip. It takes about an hour and a half.**

Girl: **I go by bike. It takes about ten minutes.**

Man 2: **I take a taxi. It's very convenient.**

DID YOU KNOW?

 In the United States, the options for public transportation [transport] really depend on the city you live in. Not all cities have a wide range of public transportation [transport] available. The New York City subway system is the only subway system in the world that runs 24/7. The London Underground, or "The Tube," is Britain's most extensive public transport system.

DID YOU KNOW?

 Some objects have a different name depending on whether American or British English is used. For example, the "subway" in American English is called the "underground" in British English. These differences can be confusing, especially when it comes to reading menus: for example, an "eggplant" in American English is an "aubergine" in British English. If in doubt, ask!

GRAMMAR

By

> How do you get to work? By bus.
>
> She goes to work by taxi.
>
> They go home by subway [underground].

On

> Do you come to work on foot?

To

Verbs such as *to work*, *to come*, *to go*, *to drive*, and *to ride* are followed by *to* + a location:

> How do you get to work?
>
> They walk to the bus stop.
>
> He drives to the station.
>
> She goes to school.

Note that *home* is an exception. We don't use a preposition with expressions such as *get home*, *go home*, *come home* and *drive home*.

> How do you get home?
>
> They go home on foot.
>
> Does he drive home?

For

> I wait for the train at the station.
>
> I'm waiting for the subway [underground].

3. **LISTENING ACTIVITY**

 Which words are missing in the following dialogues: *by*, *on*, *to* or *for*? Fill in the blanks with the correct word. If no word is needed, write "X" in the blank. Then listen to the dialogue and check your answers.

How do you get to work? Do you go by bus?

Oh, no. I don't like to wait [for] the bus. I go [by] subway [underground].

What time do you leave [   ] home?

About 8:00 or 8:15.

How long does it take to get [   ] your office?

It takes about half an hour.

Does your wife go [   ] work [   ] subway [underground], too?

No. She leaves [   ] home before 7:00. She drives [   ] work.

How do your children get [   ] school? Do they go [   ] foot?

No. They take the school bus.

174

4. SPEAKING ACTIVITY 66 99

You're chatting with a North American friend. You're curious about how she and her husband travel to their jobs in the city and how their children get to school. How do you ask her...

1. **how she gets to work?**

   How do you get to work?

2. **what time she leaves home?**

3. **how long it takes her to get to work?**

4. **if her children take the bus to go to school?**

5. **what time she and her husband get home?**

Now that you have the questions, what could her answers be?

6. **How does your friend get to work?**

   She takes the bus.

7. **What time does she leave home?**

8. **How long does it take her to get to work?**

9. **Do her children take the bus to go to school?**

10. **What time does she get home from work?**

5. WRITING ACTIVITY

Jack and Ava meet at a party. Read the information about them and then create a dialogue where they ask questions about each other's lives.

> Jack lives in the city. He works at a newspaper close to home. He could walk to work, it's only 20 minutes away. But he usually wakes up late and takes the bus, which takes about 10 minutes. He begins work at 8:30 and leaves work at 5 p.m.

> Ava lives in the suburbs. She works at a pharmacy [chemist] from 10 to 6, Monday through [to] Friday. She drives to work every day and it takes her half an hour.

Jack:

Ava:

Jack:

Ava:

Jack:

Ava:

Jack:

Ava:

Jack:

Ava:

6. WRITING ACTIVITY

Imagine you are a planning a trip to an English-speaking city. You will be staying at a friend's place, but that friend will be out of town while you are there. Write a short email to your friend to find out how to get around the town and visit the sites that you want to see.

SEND   DELETE

To:

From:

Subject:

7. SPEAKING ACTIVITY

And you? Answer the following questions.

1. **How do you normally move around your city?**

2. **Do you go by bus? By subway [underground]? By car? On foot?**

3. **How long does it take you to get to school or work?**

4. **If you go by public transportation [transport], how much does it cost you?**

5. **How long does it take you to go where you normally do your shopping?**

Check It! Test what you've learned in this lesson. Review anything you're not sure of.

CAN YOU . . . ?

☐ **talk about how you get to and from places**
I take the train, and then I take the subway [underground].
I take the bus.
I go by car to work.

☐ **talk about how long it takes you**
It takes about 35 minutes.
It takes about an hour or so.

☐ **correctly use the prepositions *by, on, to, for***
She goes to work by taxi.
Do you come to work on foot?
He drives to the station.
I wait for the train at the station.

☐ **leave out prepositions when not necessary**
What time do you leave home?

BERLITZ HOTSPOT   Go to www.berlitzhotspot.com for...

Social Networking
Do you have any experience using public transportation [transport] in an English-speaking country? Go to **Berlitz Hotspot** and tell your friends about your experiences. Share any handy tips you have.

Podcast 16
Underground Travel
Download this podcas

Internet Activity
Are you interested in more practice regarding public transportation [transport]? Go to **Berlitz Hotspot** to access the routes for the Touristic Bus in Chicago. Practice [Practise] explaining how to get from one attraction to another, using the expressions you have learned.

Video 8 – Commuting to Work
A businessman takes public transportation [transport] to work. What is his routine? How long does the commute, or journey to work, take? Watch the video and learn about the weekday commute.

Lesson 17

How Much Is the Fare?

DIALOGUE

 Listen to some tourists in New York City asking people for information about the buses.

1.

Passenger 1: **Excuse me. Does the number two bus stop here?**

Passenger 2: **Yes, it does.**

Passenger 1: **How much is the fare?**

Passenger 2: **It's two twenty-five.**

Passenger 1: **Do I need exact change?**

Passenger 2: **You need exact change or a MetroCard.**

2.

Passenger 3: **Excuse me. Which bus goes to 23rd Street?**

Passenger 4: **The number four. Do you need change?**

Passenger 3: **No, thanks. I've got a transfer.**

Passenger 4: **Good.**

1. DIALOGUE ACTIVITY

How much does the bus cost?

What is it called when you connect from one bus to another?

DID YOU KNOW?

There are different pre-paid systems for public transportation [transport] based on the city you're in. In New York City, you use a MetroCard for buses and subways. In London you buy an Oyster Card. In Sydney, you use MyZone tickets for ferries as well as trains and buses.

Use the following words and expressions to
guide you through the lesson.

VOCABULARY

avenue

can

catch

change (exact change)

crosstown

Do I need exact change?

downtown

exact

express

fare

to get off

to get on

local

MetroCard

platform

stop

to stop

ticket

transfer

uptown

Which...goes to...?

DID YOU KNOW?

In some U.S. and U.K. cities, you can purchase
one transportation [transport] card and use it
on both the bus and the subway [underground].
The card can often be refilled [topped up] at
vending machines, so you can use the same
card over and over. Discount cards are often
available for tourists and people over 65.
Often, children under 4 or under a certain
height ride [travel] for free. Visit the webpage
of the transit [transport] authority for the city
you're visiting for more information.

2. LISTENING ACTIVITY

Listen to a conversation between a man and a subway [an underground] employee. How much do you understand? Choose the correct answers.

1. **The man wants to go...**   (downtown.)/uptown.

2. **The numbers 5 and 6...**   go downtown./don't go downtown.

3. **To get to Park Street he has to take...**   an express train./a local train.

4. **The number 5 train...**   stops at Park Street./doesn't stop at Park Street.

3. LISTENING ACTIVITY

Listen to a woman in a New York subway [underground] station asking for directions to Chinatown. What directions does the man give her? Number the directions from 1 to 6. The first one has been done for you.

	Wait for the number 6 train.
1	**Wait on the express platform.**
	Get off at 59th Street.
	Take the number 4 or the number 5 train.
	Walk across the platform.
	Get off at Canal Street.

4. READING ACTIVITY

Read these three conversations about bus and subway [underground] travel. Can you fill in any of the missing words? Then listen to the conversations to check your answers.

1.

Woman: **Excuse me.** Which **bus** _____
to 10th Avenue?

Man: **You have to** _____ **the number 42.**

Woman: **Does the number 42** _____ **here?**

Man: **Yes, it does.**

2.

Woman: **Driver! Is** _____ **the bus to 34th Street?**

Bus Driver: **No. You have** _____ **take the number 4.**

Woman: **Where can I get the number 4?**

Bus Driver: **It** _____ **right here.**

3.

Man: **Excuse me, please. Is** _____ **a subway [an underground] station near here?**

Woman: **There's one at 86th Street.**

Man: **How** _____ **is the fare?**

Woman: **It's two twenty-five.**

Man: **Do I need exact** _____ **?**

Woman: **No. Just buy a** _____ **at the station.**

GRAMMAR

In American English, *have* is usually used to express possession.

We have a car.

I have exact change.

She has a bike.

He has a motorcycle.

Note: In British English, the term *have got* is often used for the American *to have* to show possession:

I've got a new car. ⟶ I have a car.

Have you got a pen? ⟶ Do you have a pen?

To form questions in the present tense with *have*, use *do/does*.

How much change do you have?

Does Ruth have a car?

In negative sentences, use *don't/doesn't*.

I don't have change.

Ruth doesn't have a motorcycle.

We use *have to* to talk about things that need to be done.

I have to wait for the bus.

He has to drive to work.

The negative forms *don't have to/doesn't have to* mean *it's not necessary. Have* in this case could also be substituted with *need*.

You don't have to buy a token.

She doesn't have to walk.

We use *can* to express possibility.

Can you drive to work?   Yes, I can.

Can I get to Park Street by bus?   No, you can't. You have to
                                          go by subway [underground].

You can buy tokens at a subway
[an underground] station.

5. SPEAKING ACTIVITY "

You're at a bus stop in San Francisco. What questions do you ask to get these answers?

1. Q: **Where does the number 42 bus stop?**

   A: **The number 42 bus stops right here.**

2. Q:

   A: **The fare is $1.75.**

3. Q:

   A: **Yes, you need exact change.**

4. Q:

   A: **No, I don't have any change.**

5. Q:

   A: **The subway [underground] station is at Market Street.**

6. SPEAKING ACTIVITY "

You have a series of questions. Can you think of appropriate answers?

1. Q: **Where can I catch the number 6 bus?**

   A: **There's a stop at the next corner.**

2. Q: **What's the closest [nearest] station to the National Gallery?**

   A:

3. Q: **How much is the fare?**

   A:

4. Q: **Do I need a ticket?**

   A:

5. Q: **Can I buy tickets from the driver?**

   A:

7. WRITING ACTIVITY

Nathan, an English-speaking friend, is planning a visit to the town where you were born. Send him an email, and provide him with the following information about your hometown: name of the town and its size, a short description of the subway [underground], bus and/or train system and the price of the fare.

✉ SEND   ✖ DELETE

To: | You
From: | Nathan
Subject: | A Visit to Your Hometown

Hi!

Can you tell me about the town where you were born? What is the name of the town? How large is the town? Can you tell me about the town's subway [underground], bus and train system and the cost of tickets?

Bye,

Nathan

✉ SEND   ✖ DELETE

To: | Nathan
From: | You
Subject: | A Visit to Your Hometown

8. ACTIVITY 📎

Now, draw a picture of your hometown, and label the main landmarks and public transportation [transport] stops for Nathan in English.

home town map

Check It!

Test what you learned in this lesson. Review anything you're not sure of.

CAN YOU . . . ?

☐ **ask about public transportation [transport]**
Excuse me. Does the number 2 bus stop here?
Which bus goes to 23rd Street?
How much is the fare?

☐ **recognize different uses of** *have*
to express possession ⟶ We have a car.

to talk about things that need to be done ⟶ I have to wait for the bus.

☐ **use public transportation [transport] expressions**
exact change
transfer
express
local
fare

 BERLITZ HOTSPOT Go to www.berlitzhotspot.com for...

Social Networking
Have you traveled [travelled] around by train? Do you enjoy taking the train? Or, if you haven't, do you think you would enjoy it?
Go to **Berlitz Hotspot** and share your experiences, preferences and plans with your Hotspot friends.

 Podcast 16
Public Transportation
Download this podcast

 Internet Activity
Plan a train trip! Choose a destination, then do a search with your favorite [favourite] search engine. What are your transportation [transport] options? How will you move from place to place? Make an itinerary. Think about how much it will cost you and how long it will take you to move from one site to another.

Lesson 18

Taxi, Please!

DIALOGUE

 Listen to some passengers in a taxi in the U.K.

1.

Woman 1:	**Taxi!**
Taxi driver 1:	**Where to?**
Woman 1:	**To Trafalgar Square, please. How far is that from here?**
Taxi driver 1:	**About a mile.**

2.

Woman 2:	**Are you free?**
Taxi driver 2:	**Yes, I am! Where would you like to go?**
Man:	**To Heathrow Airport.**
Taxi driver 2:	**Heathrow? OK. What time does your flight leave?**
Man:	**At four forty-five.**

3.

Woman 2:	**Good morning!**
Taxi driver 3:	**Good morning! Where to?**
Woman 2:	**Can you take me to the Victoria and Albert Museum?**
Taxi driver 3:	**The V&A? That's about five minutes from here.**
Woman 2:	**Good!**

Lesson 18 — Taxi, Please!

Use the following words and expressions to guide you through the lesson.

VOCABULARY

airport	museum
Are you free?	No problem.
Can you take me to...?	to owe
driver	passenger
flight	receipt
How far...?	tip
to keep	To (the)..., please.
may	Where to?
mile (1.6 km)	Where would you like to go?

1. DIALOGUE ACTIVITY

Where does each passenger want to go?

Trafalgar Square

DID YOU KNOW?

As soon as you enter a taxi, or cab, you're charged a fee, and with every set distance driven, the fare increases. You may also be charged a higher rate during peak hours and at night.

There is a "bill of rights" for taxi passengers in the U.S. Passengers have the right to pay by credit card, to specify the route, to request air conditioning or heating, to have a noise-free and smoke-free ride [journey] and more. If your cab driver provides poor service, you also have the right not to tip. Otherwise, a small tip is common.

191

2. LISTENING ACTIVITY

 Listen to a passenger taking a taxi to Macy's. Answer the questions.

1. **How long does it take to get to Macy's?**

   About ten minutes.

2. **How much is the fare?**

3. **How much does the passenger give the driver?**

Woman: **Good morning. Are you free?**

Taxi driver: **Sure. Where would you like to go?**

Woman: **To Macy's. Do you know where that is?**

Taxi driver: **Macy's Department Store? No problem.**

Woman: **How far is it from here?**

Taxi driver: **About ten minutes.**

Woman: **Good!**

Taxi driver: **Here you are. Macy's.**

Woman: **How much do I owe you?**

Taxi driver: **Four dollars.**

Woman: **Here's five dollars. Keep the change.**

Taxi driver: **Thank you.**

Woman: **Oh, may I have a receipt, please?**

Taxi driver: **Sure. Here you are, and thanks for the tip.**

DID YOU KNOW?

 Paper money is called a *bill* in the U.S. and a *note* (short for bank note) in the U.K.

Can/May I Have

We use *can* to make a request or to ask if someone is able to do something.

> Can you take me to Macy's?
>
> Can you give me a receipt?

The expression *May I have...?* is a polite way of asking someone for something.

> May I have a receipt, please?
>
> May I have the map, please?

3. WRITING ACTIVITY

Write questions based on the prompts. Use either *can* or *may*.

1. **You want the taxi driver to take you to the Natural History Museum.**

   > **Can you take me to the Natural History Museum?**

2. **You want a receipt.**

3. **You have bills [notes] only, and you want change to buy a subway [an underground] card.**

4. **You want a map.**

5. **You want to know how long it takes to get to Gatwick Airport by taxi.**

PRONUNCIATION

The *–s* at the end of words, both as a verb ending and to make plurals, is not always pronounced the same way. Listen to the activity below for examples.

4. LISTENING ACTIVITY

 Notice the spelling of these verbs. Pay special attention to the pronunciation of the final *–s* in each word. Listen and repeat each word.

s = s sound		s = z sound		s = ez sound		s sound in irregular verbs	
walk	walks	leave	leaves	close	closes	do	does
stop	stops	go	goes	use	uses	have	has

5. LISTENING ACTIVITY

 Listen and repeat the following sentences. Be sure to pronounce the final *–s* of the verbs.

My husband drives his car to work.

Linda takes the bus to school.

She leaves home at eight o'clock.

The train stops at Park Street.

My son goes to school by bike.

He gets home before three o'clock.

The Present Continuous

GRAMMAR

We use the present continuous to speak about something that is happening at the present moment, just at the moment when we're speaking.

> She's not home now. She's exercising in the park.

It is also used to express the present, but not necessarily in the same moment when we're speaking.

> Danny quit [gave up] studying French. He's studying Spanish now. (He isn't necessarily studying right now.)

We often use the present continuous to speak about a period of time in the present, for example: *the day*, *today*, *this morning*, *tonight*, etc.

> He's spending the day with his friends.

The present continuous is formed with *to be* (am/is/are) + *verb* + *-ing*.

Affirmative:	He is going home now.
Negative:	He is not going home now.
Interrogative:	Is he going home now?
Short answers: Use the corresponding form of the verb *to be* (without the verb+ -ing).	Yes, I am./No, he isn't.

Note: In spoken English, the forms are often contracted in affirmative and negative sentences.

> He's going home now.
>
> He's not going home now./He isn't going home now.

6. WRITING ACTIVITY

Read the dialogue below and fill in the missing verbs in their correct form, either present or present continuous, based on the prompts.

Woman: **Wow! It** `is` `taking` **a long time to get to the airport. (take)**

Taxi driver: **Well, there** _____ **a lot of traffic. (be)**

Woman: **How long** _____ **it normally** _____ **from here? (take)**

Taxi driver: **Twenty minutes.**

Woman: **It's already been forty-five!**

Taxi driver: _____ **you** _____ **me to take a different way? (want)**

Woman: **I** _____ _____ **.** _____ **you** _____ **it will be faster? (know (not)/think)**

Taxi driver: **Maybe. I** _____ **not sure. (be)**

Woman: **Let's try it. This traffic** _____ **not** _____ **! (move)**

7. SPEAKING ACTIVITY

Now create your own dialogue that takes place in a taxi based on the prompts.

Man: Ask if the taxi is free.

Taxi driver: Say that you are free.

Man: Ask how long it takes to get to Hyde Park.

Taxi driver: Say it takes about 10 minutes.

Man: Ask what the fare is.

Taxi driver: Give the fare.

Man: Agree.

Taxi driver: **Hop in!**

8. READING ACTIVITY

Read the dialogue and circle the correct words. The first one has been done for you.

> Where to?

> **May/Can** you take me **to**/at Fifth Avenue, please?

> Sure. Are you **coming at/going to** work?

> Not today. I have the day **out/off**.

> Oh, I see. What are **you doing/do you do** in the city today?

> I'm spending **some/these** time in museums and department stores. I'm also **meeting/making** a friend for lunch, and **we see/we're seeing** a Broadway play.

> Very nice. Do you take a taxi **to/at** work every day?

> No. I **have/take** the bus to Penn Station from the suburbs. Then I go **in/on** foot to my office.

> Oh. I drive my car to work. And then at work, I drive a taxi!

DID YOU KNOW?

The word *queue*, used in British English, is both a noun and a verb. In American English, a queue is known as a *line* and to queue is to wait in line. In both countries, it is considered very rude not to respect a line [queue].

Check It!

Test what you learned in this lesson. Review anything you're not sure of.

CAN YOU . . . ?

☐ **ask questions related to taking a taxi**
Are you free?
Can you take me to the Victoria and Albert Museum?
How much is the fare?
May I have a receipt?

☐ **understand the use of *can* versus *may***
Can you take me to Macy's?
Can you give me a receipt?
May I have a receipt, please?
May I have the map, please?

☐ **pronounce *–s* at the end of words**

walk	walks
leave	leaves
close	closes

☐ **form and use the present continuous tense**
Affirmative: He is going home now.
Negative: He is not going home now.
Interrogative: Is he going home now?
Short answers: Yes, I am./No, he isn't.

Learn More

Try to find some street, subway [underground] and bus maps for cities in English-speaking countries. Study the names of the major sites you'd like to visit, the streets on which they are located and the major subway [underground] stations. Practice [Practise] using the vocabulary you'd need to travel on public transportation [transport] to the various places.

BERLITZ HOTSPOT

Go to www.berlitzhotspot.com for...

 Social Networking
Have you ever driven in a foreign country? Was it like driving at home or did you run into problems? Go to **Berlitz Hotspot** and share your experiences with your Hotspot friends.

 Podcast 18
The Rules of the Road
Download this podcast

 Internet Activity
Are you interested in more practice? Use the internet to look up destinations in an English-speaking city. Create dialogues between you and a taxi driver. Explain to him or her where you want to go, how you want to get there, discuss the fare, ask for a receipt, etc.

 Video 9 – Taxi!
A woman needs a taxi. How does she hail a taxi? Where is she going? Watch the video and find out one way to get a taxi.

1. Circle the correct word.

1. Is there any/(a) bank near here?

2. I know his parents, but I don't like him/them.

3. The theater [theatre] is just over/around the corner.

4. I don't have any/some children.

5. His English is very good/well.

6. She's a nurse at/for the hospital.

2. Match the question words to the rest of the question.

1.	Where	a.	children does she have?
2.	What	b.	do you live?
3.	How	c.	money do you have?
4.	How many	d.	do you close?
5.	What time	e.	do I get to the bank?
6.	How much	f.	does he do?

3. Complete the sentences. Use *in*, *on* or *at*.

1. My house is [on] Park Street.

2. Turn left [   ] the first traffic light.

3. The cameras are [   ] the fourth floor.

4. There's a mailbox [post box] [   ] Seventh Avenue.

5. Her office is [   ] New York.

6. The restaurant closes [   ] 11 p.m.

7. The Palace Theater [Theatre] is [   ] the left.

8. Carol works [   ] the suburbs.

9. Don't go to the park [   ] night.

10. The bank is closed [   ] Sundays.

4. Answer the questions. Use the words in parentheses and *some, any, one,* or *none.*

1. **Is there a bus stop near here?** (on the corner) (yes)

   > Yes, there's one on the corner.

2. **Are there any department stores near here?** (no)

3. **Is there a hotel near here?** (near the post office) (yes)

4. **Is there a train station near here?** (no)

5. **Are there any supermarkets near here?** (on the next block) (yes)

6. **Are there any banks near here?** (on Main Street) (yes)

5. Complete each sentence with *by*, *on* or *at*.

1. **Do you always go to work** <u>by</u> **subway [underground]?**

2. **Can I pay** _____ **credit card?**

3. **My children go to school** _____ **foot.**

4. **The bank closes** _____ **5 p.m.**

5. **I'm paying** _____ **personal check [cheque].**

6. **The bus stop is** _____ **Park Street.**

6. Ask a question for each answer. Use the clue to help you.

1. **About a mile from here.** (how)

   How far is it?

2. **Yes. There's a bank on the next block.** (is)

3. **The dressing room is over there.** (where)

4. **I take the subway [underground] to work.** (how)

6. **The Palace Theater [Theatre]? Turn left at the corner, and it's on the right.** (how)

6. **It takes half an hour.** (how)

7. Complete each sentence with the comparative form of *good, small, long, light, fast* or *expensive.*

1. **This skirt is too short. Do you have a** longer **one?**

2. **How much are those bags? Are they** ____ **than these?**

3. **She likes her new job. It's** ____ **than her old one.**

4. **Take the express train. It's** ____ **than the local.**

5. **This car is too big. I need something** ____ .

6. **This is very heavy. Do you have a** ____ **one?**

8. Choose the correct response.

1. **Is there a bus stop around here?**

   a.   **Yes, it does.**   b.   **No, it doesn't.**   (c.)   **Yes. It's over there.**

2. **How far is it from here?**

   a.   **About 2 miles.**   b.   **Yes, it is.**   c.   **No, it's near.**

3. **What are your hours?**

   a.   **It's four-thirty.**   b.   **It's nine o'clock.**   c.   **Nine to five.**

4. **Are you free?**

   a.   **Sure.**   b.   **It's expensive.**   c.   **I'm not going downtown.**

5. **Do you take credit cards?**

   a.   **I don't have change.**   b.   **Yes, of course.**   c.   **No, we take Visa.**

6. **Do you have this sweater [cardigan/jumper] in a smaller size?**

   a.   **The vests [waistcoats] are over there.**   b.   **No, I'm afraid not.**   c.   **Every Wednesday.**

9. Complete each sentence with the correct form of the verb
in parentheses.

1. It | takes | about half an hour

    by train. (take)

2. **How do I** | | **to the bus**

    station? (get)

3. **I** | | **to work every**

    day. (walk)

4. **John wants to** | | **a new**

    suit today. (wear)

5. **The white sweater [cardigan/jumper]**

    | | **$125.** (cost)

6. **Mary** | | **at the bank**

    three days a week. (work)

10. Match the words on the left to their opposites on the right.

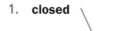

1. **closed**   a. **up**

2. **down**   b. **dark**

3. **long**   c. **cheap**

4. **right**   d. **open**

5. **expensive**   e. **left**

6. **light**   f. **short**

11. Choose the words from the box to complete each category.

~~car~~	dark	suit	~~taxi~~	bright
sweater [cardigan/ jumper]	~~airplane [aeroplane]~~	walk	short	exact change
token	check	drive	on foot	blouse

1. **train, bus, subway [underground]...**

car	airplane [aeroplane]	taxi

2. **jacket, shirt, shoes...**

3. **cash, credit card, transfer...**

4. **long, heavy, light...**

5. **ride [lift/journey], get off, get on...**

12. Complete each sentence with the present continuous form of the verb in parentheses.

1. I [am] [going] by train this week. (go)

2. John [ ] [ ] a suit today. (wear)

3. She [ ] [ ] Spanish now. (study)

4. I [ ] [ ] off at the next stop. (get)

5. Tim worked at the bank, but now he [ ] [ ] for the newspaper. (work)

6. Sharon [ ] a taxi to the airport, I [ ] the bus. (take)

Answer Key

1. Hi. Morning. Good afternoon. Hello. Good evening. Goodbye. Good night.

2. a. 4,   b. 3,   c. 1,   d. 2

3. Good afternoon.; Good, My name; sorry, please; My first, my last, is; Thank you

4. 1. M. Campana;   2. G. Chaplin;   3. P. Massey;   4. T. Bisset

5. Answers will vary.

6. Names of the women: 1. Susan; 2. Lisa; 3. Ellen; 4. Steve; 5. Paul; 6. Richard

7. Answers will vary.

8. 1. they are, 2. she is, 3. we are, 4. I am, 5. you are, 6. he is, 7. it is

9. 1. I'm, 2. we're, 3. you're, 4. he's, 5. they're, 6. it's, 7. she's

10. 1. they are not, 2. she is not, 3. we are not, 4. I am not, 5. you are not, 6. he is not, 7. it is not

11. 1. they aren't, 2. she isn't, 3. we aren't, 4. I'm not: for "I am," you cannot use the contracted form of "not.", 5. you aren't, 6. he isn't, 7. it isn't

12. 1. his coffee, Jack's coffee; 2. their table, Mary and Elizabeth's table; 3. her car, Caroline's car; 4. his book, John's book

1. Maria Garcia, Bob Stewart, Tony Davies; Maria: Spain, Bob: Scotland, Tony: Wales

2. 1. False,   2. False,   3. True,   4. True

3. 1. Hello. My name's Kenji Matsuda and I'm from Tokyo., 2. This is Tom Priest, and he's Canadian., 3. Good evening., I'm Henri Bernard and I'm from France., 4. Gina isn't Spanish; she's Italian., 5. Is Rosa from Brazil?

4. Are you, my, sorry, I am, are you, to meet you

5. Possible answers: 1. Yes, he's well., 2. I'm from (state location)., 3. No, he's not from London. He's from Australia., 4. Yes they're American./No, they're not American. They're Canadian., 5. Yes, I'm Sue Fisher./No, I'm not Sue Fisher. I'm (state name)., 6. Pleased to meet you. I'm (state name).

6. Answers will vary.

7. 1. Is Philip from New York?, 2. Is she in Spain?, 3. Are they from Brazil?, 4. Am I from France?, 5. Are we in London?, 6. Aren't you Emma Harris?

8. 1. Yes, he is./No, he's not./No, he isn't, 2. Yes, we are./No, we're not./No, we aren't., 3. Yes, they are./No, they're not./No, they aren't., 4. Yes, we are./ No, we're not./No, we aren't., 5. Yes, she is./No, she's not./No, she isn't., 6. Yes, I am./No, I'm not.

9. 1. His car is French., 2. Her first name is Emma., 3. We are not from Italy., 4. Tom is Jack's friend., 5. We aren't from North America.

10. 1. Is that David's car?, 2. Are you Spanish?, 3. Are we from Japan?, 4. Is she John's friend?, 5. Is Judy's last name Waits?

11. 1. Hello. How are you? My name's Pablo. Where are you from? I am from Madrid in Spain, 2. Hi. I am Kenji, Tony's friend. Pleased to meet you. Where are you from? I'm from Tokyo., 3. Hello. My name is Rosa and I am from Brazil. Are you English? How are you?

12.

J	A	P	A	N	E	S	E	E	O	F	H
G	O	O	D	B	Y	E	W	E	N	S	T
G	M	E	X	I	C	A	N	O	I	E	H
M	O	R	N	I	N	G	O	L	I	V	A
C	A	K	X	N	Z	N	G	I	C	E	N
A	E	M	B	F	R	N	E	D	I	N	K
N	M	N	E	E	E	E	O	E	T	I	Y
A	E	A	T	R	N	R	R	T	A	N	O
D	O	F	F	I	I	A	N	E	L	G	U
I	A	C	A	N	K	C	M	E	I	B	A
A	F	R	E	N	C	H	A	E	A	G	W
N	S	P	A	N	I	S	H	N	N	N	I

Answer Key

LESSON 3

1. Answers will vary.

2. 1. 247, 2. 8825, 3. 906, 4. 7041

3. 1. 555–9841, 2. 555–8490, 3. 555–1703, 4. 555–2941

4. 1. This is Joe, Joe Carter. My number, is five, five, five, nine, eight, four, one., 2. This is BBA, Limited. Our number is five, five, five, eight, four, nine, zero., 3. This is Judy Wells. My number is five, five, five, one, seven, zero, three., 4. This is Delta Engineering. Our number is five, five, five, two, nine, four, one.

5. Answers will vary.

6. b. New York, 8:00 p.m.; c. Tokyo, 10:00 a.m.; a. England, 1:00 a.m.

7. Answers will vary.

8. EVEning, NUMber, MORNing, SORry; goodBYE, helLO, rePEAT, good NIGHT; MEXico, TELephone, PORTugal

9. 1. same, 2. different, 3. different, 4. same, 5. different

10. Answers will vary.

LESSON 4

1. Customer 1 orders a cup of coffee and Customer 2 orders tea with milk.

2. 1. omelet [omelette], 2. cola, 3. hot dog, 4. hamburger, 5. orange juice, 6. tuna sandwich, 7. iced tea, 8. green salad

3. an omelet [omelette], a cola, a hot dog, a hamburger, an orange juice, a tuna sandwich, an iced tea, a green salad

4. I'd like a grilled [toasted] cheese sandwich and a cup of tea, please.; I'd like a baked potato with cheese, a coffee and a mineral water, please.; I'd like an omelet [omelette] and an orange juice, please.

5. Answers will vary.

6. pastry, $2.75; coffee, $1.50; soda, $0.95; grilled [toasted] cheese sandwich, $3.25; total, $8.25

7. Answers will vary.

LESSON 5

1. cheese, potato salad, onion dip; the potato salad, onion dip

2. Jane: white wine, onion dip; David: ginger ale, cheese and crackers

3. would you like some; I'm fine, What's that; It's, Would, like some; Thanks, it's

4. Sample Answers: I'd like some coffee, please.; Cream, please.; No, I'm fine, thanks.

5. Answers will vary.

6. 1. Would you like an apple?, 2. How about some cheese and crackers?, 3. How about some chips [crisps]?, 4. Would you like something to drink?, Some ginger ale?, 5. How about some salad?

7. 1. Would you like this onion dip or that bean dip?, 2. How about something to drink? This ginger ale or that cola?, 3. Would you like this tea or that coffee?, 4. How about some wine? This white wine or that red wine?

8. this, this, that, that, some, some

LESSON 6

1. postcards, a camera, maps; 85p, £150, £7.99

2. 1. a bag: customer 1, $15; 2. two candy [chocolate] bars: customer 2, 75¢/$0.75 each, 3. maps: no one, $3.50

3. 1. d, 2. e, 3. a, 4. c, 5. b

4. nice, expensive, interesting, big, small, new

5. 1. It's a red bag./That's a red bag., 2. They're blue glasses., 3. They're black cameras., 4. It's a white phone., 5. They're orange pens., 6. It's a brown bag., 7. It's a purple watch., 8. It's a green and pink cup., 9. It's a gray [grey] car., 10. It's a yellow T-shirt.

6. 1. apples, 2. pastries, 3. camaras, 4. sandwiches, 5. men, 6. maps, 7. postcards, 8. telephones, 9. watches, 10. pencils

7. 1. How much are those bags?, 2. These aren't blue T-shirts; they're black T-shirts., 3. Those camaras aren't expensive., 4. These watches are too big., 5. Those are very nice books., 6. These cellphones [mobile phones] are expensive.

8. 1. Excuse me, do you have any Spanish newspapers?, 2. Excuse me, how much is that small camera?, 3. Excuse me, could I see that pen?, 4. Excuse me, do you have any cheap cameras?, 5. Do you have any red T-shirts?

LESSON 7

1. salesclerk [sales assistant], secretary, teacher, accountant; It isn't very easy., It's interesting.

2. Jane, Linda, Robert, Judy, Steve

3. Steve: So, what do you do, Jane? Do you work in New York?, Jane: Yes, I'm a teacher., Steve: Yeah? What do you teach?, Jane: I teach Spanish in a high [secondary] school. How about you, Steve? What do you do?, Steve: I work for a computer company., Jane: Is it interesting?, Steve: Yes, it is.

4. A teacher works in a school., A secretary works in an office., A salesclerk [sales assistant] works in a department store., A nurse works in a hospital., A waiter works in a restaurant., A journalist works in a newspaper office., An actor works in a theater [theatre].

5. 1. Do; No, I work in a small store., 2. Does; Yes, he does., 3. Are; Yes, they are., 4. Does; No, she doesn't. She teaches in a university., 5. Is; No, he isn't. He's a car salesman., 6. Do; Yes, they do.

6. Nationality: French, Occupation: doctor, Employer: City Hospital

7. His name's David Forest., He's from Canada., He's a journalist., He works at ONN.

8. Answers will vary.

9. Answers will vary.

LESSON 8

1. Tony, Tony's daughter; Tony is Bob's friend., The girl is Tony's daughter.

2. 1. an engineer, 2. separated, 3. Glasgow, 4. friend, 5. has a son

3. 1. c. Does your husband work?, 2. e. What are your brothers' names?, 3. d. Does your sister have any children?, 4. f. Where do your parents live?, 5. a. How old are your children?, 6. b. What does his wife teach?

4. David: number of children, 2; number of boys, 2; ages of boys, 9 and 14; Jane: number of children, 5; number of boys, 2; ages of boys, 3 and 7; number of girls, 3; ages of girls, 5, 9 and 13

5. Sample Answer: Hi, my name's Lisa Milano. I'm thirty-five years old. I'm a waitress, and I work in an Italian restaurant. I'm married, and I have two children. My son is seven, and my daughter is nine. About another person: My husband works in a hospital. He's a doctor.

6. 1. a,   2. any,   3. a,   4. any,   5. any,   6. a

7. Answers will vary.

8. Answers will vary.

9. Answers will vary.

10. Answers will vary.

LESSON 9

1. Manchester, London, Scotland, Paris, Greenwich; an apartment, a house, a flat, a cottage

2. 1. have a, apartment, the city; 2. live in a, house in the; 3. apartment, new building, suburbs

3. are you, new house, the suburbs, large garden, new baby, children, How about, work for, live in, study

4. 1. Yes, I know her., 2. I teach it at a high [secondary] school., 3. No, I don't have it., 4. Yes, I know them., 5. Yes, they still have it., 6. I want it off., 7. Put them in the living room., 8. Yes, I speak it well.

5. in London, for a newspaper, in a small apartment

6. Answers will vary.

7. Answers will vary.

8. 1. falling, 2. rising, 3. falling, 4. rising, 5. rising, 6. falling

9. Answers will vary.

Answer Key

TEST 1

1. 1. England, 2. ninth, 3. lemon, 4. only, 5. those, 6. water

2. 1. c, 2. b, 3. a, 4. c, 5. a, 6. b

3. The order of the sentences is: 2, 5, 4, 1, 8, 3, 9, 7, 10, 6

4. 1. What time is it in Rome?, 2. What does the green salad cost?,
   3. Are those newspapers from China?, 4. I'll have some tea.,
   5. Do you have any soda?, 6. Would you like something to drink?

5. 1. woman, 2. cameras, 3. these, 4. Pleased, 5. does, 6. at

6. 1. What would you like to drink?, 2. Would you like some red or
   white wine?, 3. What's this?, 4. Would you like cream or sugar?,
   5. Would you like some cheese and crackers or some chips [crisps]
   and dip?, 6. Would you like this cheese or that cheese?, 7. How about
   some salad?, 8. What's that?

7. 1. Yes, I am., 2. No, it isn't., 3. Yes, they are., 4. Yes, he is.,
   5. No, we aren't., 6. No, you're not.

8. 1. Bill's cameras are expensive., 2. They're my friends., 3. It's Sue
   Fisher's team., 4. It's Joe's telephone number., 5. It's that woman's
   onion dip., 6. It's Judy's car.

9. 1. second, 2. woman, 3. suburbs, 4. engineer, 5. friend, 6. floor

10. 1. A secretary works in an office., 2. A doctor works in a hospital.,
    3. A waiter works at a restaurant., 4. A teacher works in a school.,
    5. A salesclerk [sales assistant] works in a (department) store., 6. A nurse
    works in a hospital., 7. A journalist works in a newspaper office.,
    8. An actor works in a theater [theatre].

11. 1. Do you have any brothers or sisters?, Yes, I do./No, I don't.
    2. Does your husband teach at the university?, Yes, he does./No, he
    doesn't. 3. Do you have any postcards?, Yes, I do./No, I don't.
    4. Is your wife a nurse at City Hospital?, Yes, she is./No, she isn't.
    5. Do they live in a small apartment in the city?, Yes, they do./No,
    they don't. 6. Where do you work?, I work (insert location).

12. 1. Where does she live?, 2. How old is she?, 3. What's her husband's
    name?, 4. How many children does she have?, 5. How old are her
    children?, 6. Where does Paul work?

Answer Key

LESSON 10

1. the post office, She needs to head to the Italian restaurant. Around the corner is the Grand Hotel. The post office is just next to it.

2. 1. bank, 2. French restaurant, 3. gas station [petrol station], 4. supermarket, 5. drugstore [chemist], 6. theater [theatre]

3. is there; there's, next, next to; there's, next to

4. Answers will vary.

5. 1. There's a bus stop in front of the department store now., 2. There's a supermarket to the right of the department store now., 3. There are some apartments next to (to the left of) the school now., 4. There's a parking lot [car park] next to the hotel now.

6. The first building is a theater [theatre]. The second building is a computer store. The third building is a department store. The fourth building is a supermarket. The fifth building is an apartment building. The sixth building is a school. The seventh building is a hotel.

7. Answers will vary.

LESSON 11

1. the ABC Theater [Theatre], Paddington Station; The theater [theatre] is relatively close by: 2–3 blocks. Paddington Station is also close by: 1 right turn and 1 left turn

2. 1. bus station, 2. post office, 3. Forest Road

3. straight ahead, blocks, turn left, second right, the corner, turn, the first right

4. Sample Answers: 1. Go straight ahead for three blocks. Turn left. Go straight. There's a theater [theatre] on the right. Turn right. Go straight. The supermarket is on the right., 2. Go straight for two blocks. Turn left and then turn right. Go straight ahead., 3. Go straight for two blocks. It's on the right., 4. Go straight ahead for two blocks and turn left.

5. 1. up, 2. past, 3. over, 4. through, 5. past; the correct order of the directions is 3, 5, 1, 4, 2.

6. 1. Don't walk to the stop [traffic] light and turn right., 2. Don't go through the park and turn left., 3. Don't go straight ahead for two blocks., 4. Don't go past the post office., 5. Don't turn right then go straight for three blocks.

7. Answers will vary.

8. Answers will vary.

1. a sports shop, a pool, the post office; The sports shop is closed Sundays and Mondays. The pool is closed Wednesday and Thursday evenings. The post office is closed on Saturday afternoons and Sundays.

2. 1. Gino's Restaurant, 2. Dickens Department Store, 3. The Pink Champagne Nightclub; The Pink Champagne Nightclub is open from 8:20 p.m. (eight-twenty) to 2:00 a.m. (two o'clock). Gino's restaurant is open from 6:30 p.m. (six-thirty) to 11:45 p.m. (eleven forty-five).

3. Flea Market: open on Sundays only, from 10:00 a.m. to 5:30 p.m.; Empire State Building: open every day, from 9:30 a.m. to 12:00 midnight; Bronx Zoo Tour: on Saturdays only, from 9:00 a.m. to 4:00 p.m.; beautiful Bronx bus tour: on Tuesdays, Wednesdays, and Thursdays, from 8:00 a.m. to 1:00 p.m.

4. 1. Is the Empire State Building open every day?, 2. Is the Flea Market open every day?/Is the Flea Market open on Saturdays?, 3. What time does the Flea Market open?, 4. What day is the Bronx Zoo Tour?, 5. How much is the beautiful Bronx tour?

5. Answers will vary.

6. Man, I hate Mondays. I am a late sleeper, so when my alarm rings at 7:00 a.m. on Monday mornings, it drives me crazy. I feel like sleeping for another four hours! But, I have to get up at 7:00 a.m., so I can take a shower, drink a quick coffee and be on the corner at the bus stop to catch my bus at 7:30 a.m. Though I don't live too far away from my job, it takes about 30 minutes to get there. I start at 8:00 a.m. Monday to Friday on the dot. I work as a secretary. I work from 8:00 a.m. to 5:00 p.m., and I have one hour to eat my lunch. I usually go from 12:00 p.m. to 1:00 p.m.; sometimes I have to go at 12, because I am just too hungry! The only good thing about starting early in the morning is that I finish early in the afternoon. In the afternoons, I usually like to take my dog to the park. We are usually there every day from 6:00 to 7:00 p.m. Sometimes afterwards, I meet up with some friends, or go to the library or maybe watch some T.V. On weekends, I like to spend time with friends, go shopping or go to the beach. I wish every day were Saturday or Sunday!

7. Answers will vary.

8. 1. Sundays, Mondays; 2. left, right; 3. Don't, park; 4. watches, fourth; 5. time, close

Answer Key

1. computers, camcorders, DVD players; yes, no, We don't know.

2. a. 1,   b. 3,   c. 2,   d. 4,   e. 5

3. 1. 6, closing, purchases; 2. shoppers, sale, off, on sale; 3. fifth, department; 4. boy, blue jacket; 5. pair, half-price

4. Answers will vary.

5. Answers will vary.

6. 1. They are buying a TV., 2. She's buying a pair of shoes., 3. She's paying for some toys., 4. He's picking out shirts.

7. are, doing; buying; do, shop; is working; doing

8. Sample Answers: 1. I am buying a computer today., 2. Is anybody helping you?, 3. I am looking for a red jacket., 4. I am paying for my purchases right now., 5. I am shopping for shoes today.

9. Sample Answers: Can I help you?, Yes, do you carry [stock] camcorders?, Yes, we do., May I see what you have?/Thanks for your help., Excuse me. Could you help me?, Sure!, I'm looking for jackets., Jackets are located in the clothing department on the second floor.

LESSON 14

1. a blouse, a jacket, a skirt; Customer 3

2. 1. try, dressing room, small, tight, bigger; 2. great, expensive, less expensive; 3. short, longer, longer, better

3. 1. more attractive, 2. brighter, 3. darker, 4. fatter, 5. greater, 6. heavier, 7. lighter, 8. longer, 9. louder, 10. narrower, 11. shorter, 12. more stylish, 13. tighter, 14. wider, 15. bigger

4. Customer 1 wants a smaller shirt., Customer 2 wants less expensive pants [trousers]., Customer 3 wants a shorter skirt.

5. 1. d,   2. c,   3. b,   4. a

6. Sample Answers: 1. The color [colour] of the first shirt is brighter., 2. This skirt is longer./The second skirt is shorter., 3. These pants [trousers] are bigger., 4. This color [colour] is lighter., 5. The second bag is bigger./This bag is heavier.

7. Yes. Do you carry [stock] jeans?; It's too expensive. Do you have something less expensive?; Can I try them on?; I like it. I'll take them.

1. 1. by credit card, 2. by check [cheque]/in cash, 3. by check [cheque]

2. one hundred one dollars, two hundred dollars, three hundred five dollars, four hundred ninety-nine dollars, five hundred seventy-five dollars, six hundred ninety-five dollars, seven hundred sixty-eight dollars, eight hundred sixty-six dollars, nine hundred thirty-nine dollars, one thousand dollars

3. Answers will vary.

4. 1. The green sweater [cardigan/jumper] is more expensive than the white sweater [cardigan/jumper]., 2. The black dress is more expensive than the pink dress., 3. The gold ring is less expensive than the diamond ring., 4. The blue suit is less expensive than the black suit.

5. Answers will vary.

6. Sample Answers: 1. I like the color [colour] blue better [more] than the color [colour] red./I like the color [colour] red less than the color [colour] blue., etc.

7. Answers will vary.

8. 1. a, 2. b, 3. a

9. Answers will vary.

1. Man 1: train + subway [underground], Woman: bus, Man 2: car; Man 1: 1.5 hours, Woman: 35 minutes, Man 2: an hour

2. 1. d, 2. a, 3. e, 4. c, 5. b

3. for, by, X, to, to, by, X, to, to, on

4. 1. How do you get to work?, 2. What time do you leave home?, 3. How long does it take you to get to work?, 4. Do your children take the bus to school?, 5. What time do you and your husband get home? 6–10. Answers will vary.

5. Sample Answer: J: Hi, I'm Jack., A: I'm Ava. Nice to meet you., J: So where do you live, Ava?, A: I live out in the suburbs. How about you?, J: Oh, I live in the city. I like it., A: Do you? And what do you do?, J: I work at a newspaper from 8:30 to 5 every day., A: Is your office in the city?, J: Yes, actually I could walk to work, but I'm kind of lazy. It takes 20 minutes on foot, but I usually go by bus which takes about 10 minutes. What about you?, A: I work at a pharmacy [chemist] from 10 to 6 every day. I go by car, and it takes me about 30 minutes. I would love to be able to go on foot!

6. Answers will vary.

7. Answers will vary.

LESSON 17

1. $2.25; a transfer

2. 1. downtown, 2. go downtown, 3. a local train, 4. doesn't stop at Park Street

3. 5, 1, 3, 2, 4, 6

4. 1. Which, goes, take, stop; 2. this, to, stops; 3. there, much, change, MetroCard

5. 1. Where does the number 42 bus stop?/Where can I get the number 42 bus?, 2. How much is the fare?/What's the fare?, 3. Do I (you) need exact change?, 4. Do you have any change?, 5. Where is the subway [underground] station?

6. Sample Answers: 1. There's a stop at the next corner., 2. The closest station is "Charing Cross," 3. The fare is £2.25., 4. You need a token or exact change., 5. Yes, you can buy tokens from the driver.

7. Answers will vary.

8. Answers will vary.

1. 1. Trafalgar Square, 2. Heathrow, 3. The Victoria and Albert Museum

2. 1. about ten minutes, 2. $4.00 (four dollars), 3. $5.00 (five dollars)

3. Sample Answers: 1. Can you take me to the Natural History Museum?, 2. Can I have a receipt?/May I have a receipt?, 3. Can you make change? [Can you change this note?], 4. Can you give me a map?/May I have a map?, 5. Can you tell me how long it takes to get to Gatwick Airport by taxi?

4. Answers will vary.

5. Answers will vary.

6. is taking; is; does, take; Do, want; don't know; Do, think; am; is, moving

7. Sample Answers: Man: Are you free?; Taxi driver: Yes, I'm free.; Man: How long does it take to get to Hyde Park from here?; Taxi driver: Oh, about 10 minutes.; Man: What's the fare, more or less?; Taxi driver: Less than £5.; Man: Ok, great.

8. can, to; going to; off; are you doing; some, meeting, we're seeing; to; take; on

TEST 2

1. 1. a,   2. them,   3. around,   4. any,   5. good,   6. at

2. 1. b,   2. f,   3. e,   4. a,   5. d,   6. c

3. 1. on, 2. at, 3. on, 4. on, 5. in, 6. at, 7. on, 8. in, 9. at, 10. on

4. 1. Yes, there's one on the corner., 2. No, there aren't any., 3. Yes, there is one near the post office., 4. No, there isn't one., 5. Yes, there are some on the next block., 6. Yes, there are some on Main Street.

5. 1. by,   2. by,   3. on,   4. at,   5. by,   6. on

6. 1. How far is it?, 2. Is there a bank near here?, 3. Where is the dressing room?, 4. How do you get to work?, 5. How do I get to the Palace Theater [Theatre] (from here)?, 6. How long does it take?

7. 1. longer, 2. more/less expensive, 3. better, 4. faster, 5. smaller, 6. lighter

8. 1. c, 2. a, 3. c, 4. a, 5. b, 6. b

9. 1. takes,   2. get,   3. walk,   4. wear,   5. costs,   6. works

10. 1. d,   2. a,   3. f,   4. e,   5. c,   6. b

11. 1. car, airplane [aeroplane], taxi; 2. sweater [cardigan/jumper], suit, blouse; 3. exact change, check [cheque], token; 4. dark, bright, short; 5. walk, drive, on foot

12. 1. am going; 2. is wearing; 3. is studying; 4. am getting; 5. is working; 6. is taking, am taking

Photo Credits

Make **Berlitz**® the first word of your second language.

Berlitz® expands your world with travel and language-learning products in hundreds of destinations and more than 30 languages.